Semisocialism,
An Alternative Government
and Economic System

Semisocialism, An Alternative Government and Economic System (Updated January, 2013)

Author: Keith B. Anderson

Self-published by Keith B. Anderson

ISBN: 978-0-692-27764-5

COPYING/DISTRIBUTING/ MARKETING RIGHTS GRANTED TO ALL:

Keith B. Anderson
P.O. Box 4051
Bluefield, WV 24701
semisocialist@yahoo.com
Semisocialist.com

CONTENTS

INTRODUCTION

As long as we are tunnel-visioned, we will accept that which is before our eyes as being the inevitable outcome of man's existence. Imagination is stymied, and our mentality and reasoning become stagnant and limited. Thus, our minds will not possess the greatest ability to reach out and explore the many other possibilities and to obtain hold of the diverse angles of deductive reasoning regarding the Herculean task of managing the affairs of man and regarding man's endeavor to concoct solutions to the problems that plague humanity in its struggle to survive and flourish.

Such is the case concerning humanity and government. Even though ideological transitions occur throughout portions of the Governed World concerning empowered administrations, too many of the Developed World's "John and Jane Does" have, through systematic coercion and peer pressure, had their minds confined in and guided through a bigoted tube directed toward egotistic acquisition of wealth and away from the humanitarian development of the potential of the citizenry's masses. It's implied that there are only two basic behemoths between which we may choose to administer to our needs: capitalism or communism. We must have one or the other, in its most reckless or oppressive form. There are no other choices, no shades of gray, to consider. And the term "socialism" is used as the monster under the bed to frighten those who have prospered under the free-market system—a call to arms against the collective incorporation and altruistic inclusion of those who have prospered not.

This book is dedicated to opening eyes to the fact that it's OK to say no to the unchecked recklessness of the free-market system and yes to its prosperity, creativity, and its multiplicity of choices.....to say no to the extreme repression of communism and yes to its equality, fair distribution, and sustentative (life-sustaining) support base. It is committed to those tired of the lies, of the narrow-mindedness, and of the stale ideologies of those in power and of those hopelessly complacent enough to remain satisfied with being led over the edge of a cliff. It is dedicated to those wishing to break away from the flock.

It does not delve into a multiplicity of statistics, nor does it render a detailed comparison to historical references. Instead, it merely gets to the heart of the matter, in the briefest and most effective manner possible. (Thus, saving you money should you decide to print it.)

I am not a student of the scholars. None of the pedantic pioneers will be mentioned here. This is a bare-bones work of common communication for the common man. I haven't been "formally educated" in how to philosophize, nor have I been educated in how to vindicate the wrongs done by the kings. If the formally educated were so superior to those of us who are not, then why have the walls of so many kingdoms crumbled under their watch? Consequently, I also haven't been educated to accept that which is before my eyes as all-perfect. I shall not genuflect before man's established temples of vanity and control.

Basically, this literary work was written in relation to the economic and political systems of America. But, to anyone in the world reading it now, take it to heart. For it is very much relevant to you as well. Even if you are not the food on the capitalistic giant's plate, you may very well be his fork and knife, facilitating his ability to consume the livelihoods of others. Learn the greater principles of life so that your actions give power to the lords of enlightenment rather than darkness.

Originally, it was my disgust and frustration with the inadequacies and ferocity of capitalism—or more specifically, the market-based economy—that led me to undertake the writing of this book. **The market-based economy—particularly, the market-based <u>social</u> <u>system</u>— is the greatest secular threat to the peace and sanctity of man.** And I was absolutely sure that, at so many points, the scheme of national operations could be vastly improved so that a policy of fairness and balance could be better cultivated. My observations now lie in your hands.

May this work communicate in all the right ways.

SEMISOCIALIST'S CREED

Government: Not only should it establish laws and delegate authority to those who shall regulate such laws, it should also establish itself as the citizenry's soundest insurance that a structure of survival shall be maintained for all. Survival can be ensured only when all of the resources, facilities and services necessary for adequate life sustentation are provided by a human management system of blind equality that is empowered to fairly distribute the essential benefits of all assets to the total populace, with its empowerment diligently maintained in order to certify the perpetuation of said assets for all future generations to come. Perpetuation can be guaranteed only when a governing body selected by the masses is allowed to control or ensure the availability of all imperative goods and services needed by society. No essential ingredient necessary for massive human existence or advancement should fall under the graces of any private concern. As the land gave birth to all of humanity, so must that which it yields be obtainable by all who dwell upon its surface. To exclude any human sole from the ingredients it renders is to violate the right of the mind and body to strive and prosper from constructive manipulation of matter created by no terrestrial man.

The resources of this world are limited. As man strives to survive, so does he endeavor to create and produce. Life without construction is existence without merit, ancestry without legacy, and posterity without heritage. Competition is the agent employed by man which renders rewards in greater quantity to those employing it best. And though it builds ability, strength, and confidence, said agent should never allow the elite of a prior generation to bequeath a legacy of inordinate wealth unto their descendants that was gathered in the absence of future soles yet to be born. As there have been more virgin resources and less human soles in the past, so will there be less virgin resources and more human soles in the future. No era of humanity should allow the private sector of a prior generation to accumulate any materialistic advantage that allows the successive descendants of a privileged elite to be geometrically enriched to the point where the successive descendants of an unprivileged mass are geometrically deprived.

There is no greater secular legacy that a prior generation of man can render unto its descendants than a benevolent and stable system of human management—one meticulously designed to preserve the purity of the environment, to ensure the security of the masses, and to lead the people unto the highroad to prosperity and progress. Such a bequeathal delivers unto humanity's successive generations a solid foundation from which to rise to whatever heights they may.

The system of management must recognize that the acknowledgement of universal truths and the holistic incorporation of these into human policy is the only course toward anthropological growth and evolution. To deny these truths is to place humanity onto a course toward deception, falsehood, and the hardships inherent therein. To fail to seek them is to remain the fool. Man is forever the creature possessing the knowledge to be the greatest fool on Earth; therefore, his spirit must never be closed to change and resolution....no matter how painful....no matter how humbling.

The system must also recognize the fact that, as individuals, we do not always make the right moves. Personal freedom accords one the opportunity to prosper, but it also allows one to fall prey to the depths of inadequacy regarding self-preservation as one navigates life's maze of options. An administrative structure which counteracts our shortcomings is the key; the fallibility of man makes it absolutely necessary. Mistakes are inevitable, but failure must become a myth, rendered inconsequential by human management engineered to compensate for individual improvidence and dedicated to ensuring that the progressive in society never repress the passive in society.

For these reasons—and upon witnessing what should by all rights be a world of peace, cooperation, and prosperity—I conclude that true progress awaits humanity only with the introduction of a clearly defined administrative system capable of accommodating all the aforementioned requirements. For these reasons...I am a semisocialist.

"Semisocialism"--What Is It?

Let us define "semisocialism" as: a system in which an elected governing body supervises the socialist distribution of essential resources and services to the citizenry, raises revenue by selling certain categories of said resources and services to the citizenry, allows the citizenry to prosper capitalistically and without further imposition of taxation in all nonessentials and in all areas of endeavor not in competition with revenue-raising, and allots a limited but equal amount of land to each adult citizen which they may control tax-free for life. Essential services such as education and health care are socialized, housing is subsidized for anyone desiring such governmental aid, and entrepreneurs purchase raw materials at a surcharged (taxed) rate from the government and may thereby transform them into marketable products and keep all profits while paying no further taxes. Private citizens purchase—also at a surcharged rate—resources, agricultural products, and certain services from the government for their own use. Also, all utilities are under government control and are billed at a surcharged rate. In short, it can be said that semisocialism is the socialist distribution of humanity's essentials and the free-market distribution of its luxuries or nonessentials. Within its matrix, the governmental employment-and-opportunity sector expands in proportion to the private sector's inability to meet the people's needs and desires in employment and opportunity. Thus, should the private sector properly expand in its ability to provide adequate employment and opportunity in the areas in which it is allowed to participate, then the governmental sector shall back off in its penetration of the free-market arena in all said areas.

But my intended type of semisocialism is more than just a mechanical system of fair resource distribution. My version also harbors spiritually uplifting qualities by the fact that it stresses harmony with nature, incorporates the evolution and unity of humanity, and adheres to the cosmic and universal truths that shape the destiny and morality of man. It is a system that chooses to recognize these truths—the effects of population and poverty, the search for life's meaning, our common ties, etc.—and to constructively accommodate them rather than ignore them and suffer from their impending consequences. In essence, it is an administrational matrix that shall never be closed to discovery, acceptance and growth.

Because my semisocialist model seeks to incorporate all factors which affect man and because its socioeconomic aspect is geared to ensure the survival of all citizens, we may expand the term by referring to it as "holistic-humanitariansitic semisocialism" (h-h semisocialism). Still, another option—"holistocracy"—would imply: a system of human administration incorporating all known influential factors affecting earth and man and administering them for the good of earth and man. But let us reduce our options to one and refer to ourselves as "holistocratic semsocialists."

Holistocratic philosophy believes in being real with what man is—the all of man. And either we accept that which is real and incorporate it into our structure on a constructive basis, or we deny that which is real and suffer from the hand of its impending consequences. Humanity must deal with the full, deep meaning of being human, utilizing it as the fact sheet with which to gauge and mollify our shortcomings. Putting a bandage on the effect instead of a cure on the cause leaves the body's internal mechanisms tainted with systematic poison and self-destructive infections.

The empowered and affluent beneficiaries of the structural order will bandage the effects and laud this action in the utmost publicized manner, doing so in order to lure public scrutiny away from the status quo that has given them society's pedestal position. The bandages become distracting patches of decay and deterioration, covering the external surface but hiding the infection that occurs within. But, if there is to be true health and healing within the human structural order, then man must continually search his conscience, and, when it is warranted, come to say, "Maybe I'm wrong." Then, he must never be ashamed to throw down his robes of superiority, don the ones of the paupers, and beg to be saved from himself. Life is a learning process, complete with incessant tests of human capability and fallibility. And though it is uncertain whether or not we are wrong when we step off into planned directions, we are definitely wrong when we ignore the dead carcasses which lie in the wake of the actions that those directions have compelled us to take.

Certain universal human factors must be considered when establishing a civilization, especially those dealing with the darker side of man. The vices of greed, intolerance, and exploitation must bear the main yoke of regulation within a structural order designed to cancel their prominence—that is, if man is to say he is truly civilized. Otherwise, he's an ideological catastrophe waiting to happen. Holistocratic intelligence knows what man is capable of, acknowledges its inevitability, and then takes the necessary steps to lock him down.....to refrain from allowing him to run free and reckless through the candy store of planetary resources...or roughshod through the sacredness of human rights and liberties inalienable to us all. But it also is aware of the good side and pursues every avenue possible in order to allow those benevolent areas to flourish.

By examining all major universal factors—both the beneficial and the detrimental—and incorporating them into an administrative scheme which enhances their advantages and rectifies their detriment, not only does mankind display evidence of collective responsibility, he also provides the individual with a support system that creates a climate of amiability when dealing with fellow human beings, stimulating positive affections in the process. Such considerate and insightful initiative uplifts the human spirit and makes a citizenry proud to hold allegiance for a government and for a nation.

Chapter 1

SEMISOCIALIST MORALITY & PRINCIPLES

Though the term "morality" normally tends to conjure thoughts along the lines of religious adherence, abstinence, inoffensive language, and honorable conduct regarding how one accommodates one's needs and wants, the gist of semisocialist morality is concerned with man's progress and prosperity with respect to how he affects the natural environment and with respect to the collective status in which he leaves his fellow men in his endeavor to achieve his goals. The semisocialist mentality isn't concerned with whom you are sleeping; its concern is whether or not you have a bed to sleep in. Its worry isn't about what one drinks or what one sniffs or injects as much as it's concerned with whether or not one's chemically influenced state poses a danger to others, whether or not one can receive treatment if one needs it, or whether or not one's neighborhood offers fair opportunity for a better life. It doesn't care about alternative lifestyles in beach houses; it just doesn't want the beach itself—nor its surrounding water—contaminated or destroyed with waste or discarded material coming from those beach houses. Whatever other factors of judgment one wishes to consider along moral lines is between oneself and one's associates or god.

Beneficial—or, at least, innocuous—interaction is the central element constituting morality in semisocialist terms. Moral interaction preserves the environment and elevates or sustains mankind collectively; immoral interaction diminishes the environment and debases humanity collectively or in sectors. And since interaction among humans is the dominant factor affecting the whole of planetary occurrences, the relationship between the players of mankind's world stage is what we must be most concerned with. The relationship must be benevolently engineered in order to create a harmonious balance between said players and the world in which they dwell. Let us start by identifying and defining said players—the "progressionists," passivists, and the primitivists. In a nutshell, we'll define "progressionists" as the ones wanting the better mousetrap or the ones wanting more mousetraps to be made and desiring to prosper greatly therefrom. They're the ones spurring the technology or advancing or mastering the processes which dictate our present and future interactive habits. They either make the world or shake the world, acquiring much of the world for themselves in the process. Passivists—or conformists, if you wish—are the John and Jane Does sector. A pejorative term one may choose to give them is "pawns." They're the soldier ants in the progressionists' war of world dominance. Their main goal is to sustain livelihood or acquire wealth by dutifully accommodating the status quo until they may one day take their leave, hopefully on a financially secure basis. This sector also includes portions of the governmentally dependent as well as the homeless. In essence, we'll define passivists as those who exist without spurring significant change—though, we'll have to admit, there are thin lines separating marginal progressionists from marginal passivists. Lastly—and most easily to define and identify—we have the primitivists. These are the peoples who live as their ancestors have lived. We see them on TV everyday in their villages and huts. And, for all practical purposes, we'll also categorize these as ones who interact only marginally with progressionist society, living the more simple, isolated lives. Cultures dwelling on reservations may also contribute to the makeup of this group.

The progressionists must be extremely careful in all their planning as to how they affect the less catalytic categories of humans. All three human types serve important functions: progress, support, and resource conservation respectively. The progressionist's moral responsibility is to initiate only that progressive action which allows the passive sector to be maintained on an equitable basis and allows primitive culture to co-exist as genuinely undisturbed as possible within an ever-changing world. Consequently, the moral responsibility of the passivist is to strive to economically and laboriously support all progressionist endeavors which are moral and universally beneficial and to avoid and abandon those which are not—to serve as the right arm for positive change. The central moral responsibility of the primitivists is to preserve, as much as possible, the environment which sustains them.

Every step man takes to advance his knowledge, every policy he establishes—be it social, economic, or scientific—is basically an experiment into new directions....which, in the long run, may result in burning his materialistic and philosophical house down in the future just as well as it may seem to build it up in the present. In view of the inescapable fact that mankind bears many faults and cannot help but inadvertently incorporate them into any experiment he undertakes, it is imperative that certain allowances are made which create a comfort zone—a safety net—capable of serving as a buffer zone between harmonious socioeconomic equity and inflammatory socioeconomic disparity—i.e., the passivists will not remain "passive" very long if their livelihood is threatened. Also, it is absolutely essential to have a natural (primitive) resource to refer to for the purpose of observation and education—a reference to examine to see nature in an undefiled state and how progressionist man can better improve himself. The safety net must especially encompass the progressionists and passivists because it must allow them leeway to cooperate and work out their problems within their own environment, leaving the primitive environment unscathed from the "societal experiment" so that the perennial human social and environmental patterns are always pure and ready for referral should said experiment need original and unaltered input from the perennial forces of nature.

We'll now dwell on the two human types possessing the most potential for imposing world change: the progressionists and passivists.

Probably the most important question a people should ask when developing a civilization is, what if there is failure? "What if some of us fail in this game called life? Will they have enough to feed their families? To shelter them? To keep them warm in the winter?" In order to establish the strongest infrastructure possible, a society must base its administrative foundation on addressing and managing the negatives that the experiment may incur with the same—if not greater—intensity with which it addresses the positives it hopes to achieve. The reason is obvious: The positives are blessings which can only bring good. But the negatives, if left unchecked, can escalate into a state of societal deterioration and revolt. Such is the critical importance of the safety net—to support all citizens who are unsuccessful at navigating themselves through the established socioeconomic system to sustentative comfort or wealth. And the best net possible is one emanating from an administrative system which combines the ingredients of fair wealth-distribution and economic stability into a platform engineered to eliminate all imbalance of opportunity which could possibly spur the potential for socioeconomic failure. This system can function properly only by operating in an automatic and complete mode which anticipates inequities and shortcomings ahead of time and incorporates built-in solutions automatically—with no need to bandage the effect rather than cure the cause. In essence, the general socioeconomic system itself must serve as the net of safety, constantly preventing painful economic imbalance simply by the preventatives inherent within its normal, perennial operations—a system that takes into account the various motivations and individual psyches which make up the people as a collective whole. Unanimous socioeconomic health is a dish best served as the main course.

In the Modern World, all must interact with the economic system, either in a leadership or a servile basis. Those who will not make any attempt to progress their abilities—other than the amount required for employment—should not have their survival jeopardized because of their inertness. However, the human type in search of the gold and/or human advancement should be allowed to pursue such things—but only to the point where their actions do not endanger the existence of those who are not. The drones, for example, will handle the routine duties prevalent in the governmental and commercial sectors of a society. They are the ones who may labor for a designated number of years, with no further ambition other than reporting to the job and performing adequately enough to maintain it until retirement. But the individuals who branch out and exploit all their potential are our real producers. And they should be rewarded with all the feasible luxuries they deserve, for they will create the world's great civilizations.

And these civilizations must treat their citizens like cherished children, not as though they are merely faceless statistics and taxable prey. At its best, an administration will urge the citizenry onward and upward, with its arms outstretched underneath, ready to catch those who fall. At its worst, it will destroy motivation by greed or oppression and will fragmentize its people into a state of alienation and of complacency toward the value of life. This is why I could never advocate the rigid confinement of communism or the avaricious deregulatory precariousness of capitalism. I would want my children to have all the motivation they need in order to bring out the full creative brightness in themselves, yet, just because they came home with a bad financial report card, I wouldn't wish them relegated to sitting at the back of the class with little hope of ever moving forward. Nor would I want my children sitting malnourished and unfulfilled at a table of plenty.

With economic health comes societal health in general. When economic descent and destitution are a possibility, the detrimental psychological effects serve to hamper and decrease the number of clear and content heads in a society. When the economic environment suffers anxiety and doubt, it begins to prey on the mind, especially when one considers the fact that one could drop to the same social level as the "bum" one just passed by on the street. And then society must contend with all the psychological "abnormalities" as a consequence of this fear of uncertainty. Of course, there are always those who will be in a position to prosper no matter the financial situation of the little man. These will be the ones blessed with control of the basic essentials that must be bought in spite of the hardships in other areas of the economy. And, in these times, economic gaps between the rich and poor grow large.

But let those gaps become too large, and the multitude of minds can be stirred into massive aggression and rebellion.....especially in any country that stresses the free-spirit, get-mine-or-else attitude of divisive capitalism. If man doesn't perpetuate a system that accommodates adequate civilian survival, then "fights for life"—be they big, be they small—are the next, inescapable natural step. In vulnerable economic atmospheres, these "life fights" may be as subtle as the embezzler who must feed a family, pay a mortgage, send a kid to college, or simply maintain his addictive lifestyle. In austere atmospheres, they will become as volatile as the terrorist group in an urban building upwards to a seceding army in a civil war.

Land

Whenever revolutionary social confrontations occur, and whenever large or small individual wars are waged for survival, there is one prize that is the greatest prize of all: control of land—be it directly or indirectly targeted. Whether our individualistic battles center around acquiring a fair share of the money or our united wars are about obtaining a state of self-determination, both goals are obtainable only as a result of exploiting the properties of the ground beneath us. All who live and breathe on this gigantic spinning mud ball have a right—a limited right—to the land. It was in existence eons before any life form evolved to the ability to partition it off with fences and certificates of "ownership." No one asked to be born, yet 99.9% of us harbor a fear of dying that makes us strive for life. Without land, how can there be life at all—progressive or nonprogressive? We all must exist within a space, and society cannot allow its livable areas to become monopolized if it wishes to maintain domestic peace.

Let's hop into an imaginary spaceship and take a trip to far-away planet. We'll carry along and drop off one thousand unrelated humans to its surface when we get there. The planet has just one tropical strip of land capable of sustaining our thousand transplants. We'll survey it, border it off, and give each individual the equitable amount they need for survival. We'll supply them with all the agricultural tools and bodily comforts they need. And to simplify the illustration, we'll determine that procreation isn't a factor.

In this situation, it would be an intrusion for Khalid to plant part of his crop or to build part of a structure upon any of Ezekiel's lot without permission. Regardless of Khalid's goals, a fair, life-sustaining balance has been set. And, as long as its guidelines are respected, then life will remain smooth and tranquil. But any acts of aggression to unfairly expand boundaries—whether initiated by a collaborating majority or by an individual—can only resulting in heated conflict. Because the partitioned amounts of the land is the equitable amount to sustain life, to exclude any party from their granted amount would bear the potential to bring out their animalistic traits and self-preserving retaliations against their trespassers (and possible a minority sector against each other if a majority sector is the infringer and it is too powerful to fight against).

Land is an absolutely essential commodity. And since gravity naturally binds all matter to the surface of the earth, ownership of the lateral surface is a most precious possession, for it and its underside contain all essential ingredients necessary for life. Verticality is beneficial as long as it increases productivity, capability and livelihood. But, when applied as a method of "elevation and elimination," it becomes an avenue through which the economically empowered can enclave and debase a massive portion of a sector of people....effectively getting them "out of the way" of the big game going on at ground level.

In certain demographics, the market-based economy has done a splendid job of allowing the economically blessed to monopolize massive amounts of fruitful lateral land while building a subjugated and dependent vertical population, most particularly in impoverished locales. And the effects of this unfulfilled dependency can be seen in jails and on the mean streets every day. The big cities: here, we have the most expensive real estate in the world. A few billionaires and millionaires are liable to own massive portions of it. The bulk of the urban epicenters wallow in man's concrete and towering structures instead of in nature's soil and mountains. Of these epicenters, ambitious man has designed virtually every nook and cranny of them, and, as a result, has also inadvertently spread his artificial impurities through conditions of total currency dependency within a precarious system and also through the subsequent debilitating plagues of inadequate opportunity and employment, rampant crime, and crowdedness—so prevalent in the poorer sections. The affluent sect may see the lowest class as eyesores whom life has been "wasted" on and who serve as dilutions and distractions from the beauty and tranquility of their grand metropolis. Those suffering at the lower end of the spectrum may in turn regard the affluent as vultures whose only purpose is to devour every amenity for themselves and lock the poor forever outside the gates of prosperity.

But, whatever the war between the rich and poor, we can never stray from the dominant issue: Access to lateral land is at the base of all economic establishments and classes. And, in all fairness, if the wealthy were more stringently required to compensate the public for excessive lateral land usage, then the benefit of the nation's resources could be more ubiquitously distributed, allowing more pathways for more "wasted lives" to find greater opportunities to become "justified" in living.

As money may be substantiated by precious metals, people must be represented by land.....either by actual land ownership or by compensation for the benefits extracted from it. Those who are represented will bear greater chance of acquiring society's highly sought prestige of self-sufficiency. Those who are shut out are relegated to the confines of society's devalued status, bereft of a huge asset with which to tap into society's credit and profit-generating machine. Thus, when one runs this train of thought through the mind, one would have to conclude that, if a citizenry desires a society of balanced living standards, then a citizenry must uphold a system of equal land distribution.

At this point, one's mind may be formulating an opinion of: "There are those who are industrious and who will accomplish things with the land; there are those who are lazy and who won't." But understand, we cannot entertain this train of thought without accommodating a bigger-fish-eating-smaller-fish mentality—a cannibalistic sentiment that traumatizes and depreciates the value of life. If one is sitting on one's porch on one's land rocking the time away, one certainly couldn't stomach the idea of a bigger fish taking it all away just because it is more vital and energetic. Besides, just because some are passive today doesn't mean they'll be that way tomorrow. Holding control of land will allow them to have opportunities for flashes of creativity throughout their entire lives. Plus, there is also the possibility that the highly industrious may in some ways be contaminating the environment and populace with their activities even though we may consider these activities advantageous and progressive for humanity at the time. By limiting land ownership, those physical and philosophical contaminants themselves are more limited, providing us with more people approaching their goals from many more diverse angles, allowing us to learn from a broader base so that we may examine the data to achieve more innocuous results at another time. And, with all the above, there is the commercial factor that a stable consumer base must always be maintained that will patronize and utilize all advancements made by the progressionists so that they may prosper from their accomplishments.

The process which brings new life into this world was designed by forces far greater than any of us. We have nowhere near the moral right to abduct or interfere with the covenant that compliments it, that facilitates the sustaining of that new life. Simply put, no one has the right to own an excessive amount of land because no one owns life's cycle. Private entities haven't the justification to determine for the public which new life has a right to arrive, where it has a right to dwell, how it shall live, or whether it should have more of a right than others to succeed and flourish. No terrestrial being has a right to confiscate the necessities, abilities, and ambitions of the future generations and encase them inside a capsule and rule over them as well as all their feet stand upon.....not simply on the prodigiously weak argument that life's cycle brought them into the world first.....not in any argument that anyone can formulate. Yes, you may indeed have worked very hard to acquire the abundance you have now, but the future soles yet to be born haven't yet had that chance—and will have increasingly less of a chance as more and more land and resources come under the control of the elitist class of all prior generations coming before them. As these future citizens check into "Hotel Life," they have a right to have their rooms reserved in advance.

Of course, land control must be regulated. And it goes without saying that the unborn and the soles yet to be conceived cannot accomplish this. But, if the land arrangement is made intolerable by any prior generation of man, then the future generation of man will change what the prior one has established—be it through diplomacy, be it through aggression. The capriciousness and precariousness of mankind facilitates a constant shifting in conditions which perpetuates changes in the status and living conditions of all involved. One must understand that, whatever distributional policies that the prior ancestors established for themselves, their descendants may not see fit to uphold them if situations change to accord certain parties too much advantage over other parties. Thus, they may struggle and fight for a new set of conditions. And they will feel very justified—justified because they themselves had no say in determining the ingredients of the original setup. Concerning the status quo, no one likes being powerless forever—whether the existing arrangement was conceived or negotiated by their own ancestors or not. Power and its benefits must be shared or it will be taken back and forth.....with rivers of bloodshed as the common grounds of exchange more often than not.

The only way to greatly nullify all justification for future generations to engage in traumatic conflict over property is to establish a permanent system by which land is distributed fairly. And "fairly" can only mean <u>equally</u>. A system that allows equal access to the land is a nearly indomitable foundation upon which to build a society. It is virtually permanent for the simple reason that none can morally argue against the right of all to hold land and thus would be justifiably ridiculed as villains should they attempt to overturn the system which upholds that equality. Secondly, with equal land access being in effect, this eliminates a big potential grievance for the populace to bring against the establishment. However, if it is the governmental administration that is the intolerable element, then equal land ownership, even if in effect, may do little to stem the violent tide of those harboring an overwhelming desire for systematic revision. But the most dangerous culprit which stirs the general populace into violent confrontation is the lack of adequate access to necessities for survival. And a correct policy of property distribution would serve to negate much of the anger directed against the establishment for its inadequacies and infringements due to the fact that the land bearing the sustentative necessities is evenly dispersed to the control of the masses. All in all, holding a piece of property one can call one's own just gives one a plain, good feeling. And people who "feel good" seldom feel the need to resort to harming anyone.

Resources

An enormous quantity of elements and compounds are spread out in various types and in diverse amounts wherever one treads upon the earth. Some of us are blessed with more significant portions than others. But, as we are all living organisms, our biological functions are in constant operation and their needs must be met and served. They are in operation regardless of the quantity of resources in our general locales and regardless of the fact that there will always be more capable individuals than ourselves with greater intellectual ability to manipulate those resources in order to extract the most benefit from their properties. There will always be those who are more intelligent than ourselves and who are our seniors in age. But, whatever relationship we may hold with one another, NO ONE OWNS LIFE'S CYCLE! There will always be those who will try, but they will always be dealt a crushing blow in the end.

Like land, resources were in existence for time immemorial before God or fate chose to give life's cycle the OK to bring any of our particular selves upon the earth. They were not instantaneously provided upon the appearance of any specific human or humans. We all need access to the benefits of resources or we cannot live. Since no one owns life's cycle, no one has the right to determine who does or does not deserve sustentation, and therefore, no one sector of people has a right to draw up "pretty papers" and take all from another sector.

Those who are more economically competitive and "more intelligent" should not be allowed inordinate control over the resources, not only because of its detriment to equality, but also for the reason that those who own the resources hold control over those who need them. Those who are at their mercy will be forced to directly or indirectly shape their lives around the motivations and grand schemes of the power elite. Excessive resources in only a few hands is power. Power in the wrong hands does indeed corrupt, as seen in all too many cases throughout history. And the best way to reduce that corrupting agent is to dilute its ability to occur by more equitably distributing the elements that it occurs by. This also diminishes the devil's workshop of idleness by allowing the people access to more elements to creatively exploit as individuals.

There will always be a prior generation. And even though there can be no moral gluttony of the resources by that generation, there must be moral regulation of Earth's gifts by that generation. If there is to be a tranquil future for mankind, we must come to understand that the ultimate responsibility of all existing generations regarding the things of the earth is to ensure their equitable accessibility to the existing masses and to strategically extract them from nature's grasp—recycling them as much as possible—so that the future generations' fair share will never be transgressed.

Space exploration: Here, we must accommodate the most critical management of resources. There is little margin for error; there is limited space aboard ship to exploit. Everything must be planned and designed for maximum efficiency. The ship has been engineered for greatest power and function. The life aboard it is precious—nurtured and trained with great care. That same precious life is not denied any resource it needs in order to survive or succeed in its mission. There is no room for greed, no room for deprivation. All cohabitants must operate in cooperative unity. Everyone is held in significant esteem. If only we would invest the same care and consideration in designing our terrestrial support systems as our scientists do in the planning of our cosmic ones.

Nature

As land and resources are the base and vital elements necessary to maintain all life, nature is the covenant which sustains and replenishes the resource and base and which dictates the activities of all life. As long as the rules regarding its countenance are accommodated, it will provide us with all we need and more. But, if violated, its retaliatory effects can traumatize and punish man with deficiency, defilement and pestilence.

It requires foresightful and benevolent planning to remain within the guidelines of nature. But our industrial nations have fallen tragically short of this nobleness. Greed, waste and haste have corrupted all human planning.

And the Mother of the Earth holds no place for these detrimental traits if she is to forever provide us with a wholesome environment. We fail to uphold her standards and she holds the mirror of evidence up to our faces, in which we see the reflections of our faulty endeavors in the form of chemically contaminated rivers and streams of dead fish, smoke-filled air which deteriorates our lungs, disappearing wildlife, and high rates of cancer in residents near facilities storing hazardous waste and materials. Instead of powering our homes, vehicles and machines with what she gives so freely— the sun, the wind, the water—we choose to keep our purses enslaved to the barons hoarding the fuels, further destroying our world, and forever pitting brother against brother. And, last but certainly not least, let us never forget what is probably the most ominous mirror of all, the ever-prevalent global warming.

Nature is a strict mother, but she is also a loving mother. She holds the evidence up to our eyes, not to deflate our egos, not to belittle our spirits, but to warn her human children when they are wrong—to discipline them to change their ways. We must change our ways because we failed to listen when she rendered her first speech, a speech that showed us how to live before we began our cataclysmic march toward the defilement of her body. And that speech was one of socialization.

One of nature's greatest attributes is that it is indeed socialized. All carbon-based organisms may not bear this trait, but their support base—the water, soil, and atmosphere—is definitely a conglomerate of ardent practitioners. Upon activation by the sun, vapor rises from the waters, inhabits and condenses in the atmosphere, and descends to the ground. The land is then enabled to produce vegetation, which not only sustains animal life and decays into soil, but which also releases oxygen.....reactive with hydrogen.....and we return to the waters. All these elements must work in conjunction. None can sustain from sharing their attributes or life's cycle as we know it will cease to exist. But not only does our loving mother propagate socialization through Earth's elements and vegetation, she also supports its practices in the way man himself is designed. He must breathe oxygen, drink water, and eat—be the sustenance vegetation or flesh. He even participates in the perpetuation of the cycle by providing plants with carbon dioxide through his exhalations. And nature so earnestly desires us to adopt a philosophical connection to compliment the physical one that we already share with her elements.

We must treat our environmental mother like the life-generating organism that she is, never letting our artificial experiment overtake and defile her metabolic chemistry. We have come to rely too heavily upon the inferiorities of mankind's theoretical and immature conceptions rather than upon the superiority of nature's perennial and exemplary teachings. We must adapt— or evolve—to emulating nature's cycle and allow it to develop us through the correct modes of existence. It must become the physical educator that exemplifies the correct and wholesome way of life—one of mutual cooperation, one of sharing life-giving resources.....one of socialization. It must become the dictator—a cherished and guarded dictator—which mankind diligently obeys, which decides when we have acted too irresponsibly and have surpassed the safety factor necessary for a safe world regarding the facilities we build, the mechanisms we create, or the environmental actions we take.

Another of nature's greatest attributes is the fact that it's chemically holistic. Every molecular component is there, every ingredient we need to evolve and advance into whatever superior stage we are to reach. The evolutionary forces of nature are infinitely superior to man's conceivable intellect. When these forces are respected and benevolently incorporated, the lot of mankind stands the greatest chance for peace and contentment. The rush and struggle to correct man's ecological mistakes and to find the treatments for related ailments would be eliminated. Man could <u>slow down</u>.....and be kinder to himself..... because the resulting abundance of material things would ameliorate the competition for materialism as well as for survival.

If only we would walk instead of run. If only we would behave ourselves and eat our vegetables like good little boys and girls, Mama Nature would give us what we need as well as what we want <u>when</u> she feels we're ready. Yes...if only we had checked with her first...let <u>her</u> be our teacher and leader, and we treated her with honor and respect—as we should have always treated one another. There would have never have been such a need to correct so many developmental errors and shortcomings. Our scientific, technological, and economic pursuits could have been dedicated more so to making our <u>good</u> lives <u>better</u> than to just making our <u>fair</u> lives <u>bearable</u>. But, we little children didn't choose to sit down and let Ms. "N" teach her class, did we? And we still refuse to hear her lectures today as she continuously tells us what's wrong over and over again. We get an "F." And we'll continue to fail the class until our geed and reckless ambition give way to sense, patience and obedience.

Yes, the Mother of the Earth would give us everything. Most graciously, she would render unto us the greatest process of evolution in which we could actively participate—a process made possible only by our dedication to remain within her guidelines as we advance from stage to stage. We evolve because, when we dedicate our homage to Earth's most superior systematic setup, it works <u>with</u> us, sending its invigorating forces throughout our bodies to sustain vital health and throughout our minds to progressively stimulate our intellect. We receive the purest of nourishing evolutionary forces, most of which we have never discovered and may never truly understand, but forces which our natural parent will give willingly, continuously, and absolutely without any deleterious side effects such as those brought about by man's artificially imposed haste. We also evolve because, when we follow our Mother's ways of socialization, we honor ultimate respect for human need. And our ideological motivation becomes dedicated to heading off the most detrimental humanistic traits which jeopardize it: Gluttony, environmental destruction—these stumbling blocks would be "morally outlawed" in the classroom and courtroom of Mother Nature. But when her statutes are violated and thrown out of balance, the body of man, the mind of man, and the morality of man are contaminated with poison, trauma and malevolence. The stumbling blocks become active in massive force. Gluttony leads to environmental plundering. Now man must hurry to find new usable land space, additional resources, new energies, new sources of food and water, to control pollution, to replenish vanishing forests and threatened animal species, and to curb the ailments resulting from the man-made imbalance.

And because only a few can be blessed with excess, many of the remaining mass will dwell in the realms of deficiency—which, as we all know, can only lead to a society crumbling from within, by systematic failure, dissention, or both. Thus, instead of mankind connecting with the forces of nature in rewards of human elevation—humanitarian evolution—he collides with <u>himself</u> in animosity and destruction. And often the end result is the rebuilding of his rubble without the reshaping of his priorities.

The mother will correct her systems in her own way no matter the actions of man. Even if we succeed in destroying a significant portion of her present life forms—and ourselves in the process—she will purify and reinvent herself, reemerging with a new and/or altered set of organisms given the right to approach life under terms maybe bizarre to ourselves. But, while we are here and have the capacity to correct ourselves, we can prevent nature's exemplary cycles from suffering damage because of our ill-conceived actions—and therefore avoid retribution unleashed by the forces surrounding us. We will lose so much if we don't—so much so fast before we even know it. Many vegetative and animalistic organisms suffer injury to a point where they arrive at extinction levels, sometimes even before being discovered by human eyes, thereby wiping out any chance of our reaping the benefits they may have given us.

Though nature's countenance on the earth is indomitable, its cyclic setup is extremely delicate. All lower life forms will adhere to and be regulated by the laws and guidelines of nature purely by instinct. But man must rely on his own sentient logic, and only he can prevent his kind from drastically disturbing the cyclic balance. It doesn't require every human to be destructively active before damage is imposed upon our support systems. Only a handful of people own and control the factories, chemical plants, logging businesses—conveniences from which a great deal of the world doesn't even benefit. Indeed, the earth itself didn't have to be completely covered with our pesky little selves before it began rebuking our presence. If 7.1 billion humans were put into one location, with each given four square feet of standing room, they would all fit into an area of only 1,033 square miles—roughly 32 X 32 miles. Because we humans—even in the smallest of numbers—bear such a great potential for contaminating the world system, and because no singular or few sole(s) can accumulate the facilities necessary to wreak havoc upon our environment if the whole of society refuses to allow it, the whole of man must stand accountable for the actions of every man in the courtroom of nature. The mirror of evidence is the judge and jury.

Education

Once the rules are set in place regarding the respect for land distribution, resource accessibility, and for nature's countenance, the minds of the citizens must be trained to manipulate those areas to their and society's greatest advantage. That advantage can only be pursued when the society determines specifically the abilities and talents that it needs to extract from its citizenry in order to fulfill its needs and wants. The ultimate point: In order for the whole of society to remain vitally active, it must establish a place for each and every individual to contribute to its prosperity. The specific individual occupations and their needed quantity can only be determined through meticulous planning by insightful administrators. But the occupational training awarded to each individual citizen can best be determined through testing of the scholastic achievements of the person. And the level of fairness by which all of society's populace is given equal access to the highest achievable levels of opportunity dictates the level of vitality, creativity, and success with which that society will be blessed.

The struggle to meet the financial burdens of furthering one's higher education is a worry upon the mind....a worry which can prove to be detrimental to the brain's ability to intake instruction.....a worry which can prove to be realistically tragic by the inability of the individual to meet those financial obligations. No person—who is capable, willing, and who will live a life of significant length—should be forced in any way to forego pursuit of an occupation just because they are financially unable to fund the training it requires, especially training regarding occupations which have been determined to be critically needed nationally. In all practicality, all financing of education in essential fields should be accommodated by the government. It's simple: If a society's future needs are for agricultural experts, then it should "pay" for agricultural experts. If it needs more doctors and teachers, then it should fund the training of more doctors and teachers. It is nonsensical to force any individuals of such potential or their parents to expend time and effort gathering the resources necessary to buy the "ticket" so that they may pass through the gates of education on their way to sustaining and advancing a nation. This is especially true of nations with a comfortable supply of resources and/or harboring lucrative industrial capabilities. The finance is already there for education. All that's needed are prudent administrators capable of extracting the fiscal benefits of those resources so that the needs and talents of the potential graduates can be fulfilled and nurtured.

However, before we can rise up to the more complicated, adult levels of occupational training and materialistic acquisition, the most important developmental stage for all of us is our period from infancy through early childhood. In infancy, if adequate oxygen supply is prevented from reaching the brain, then we face a lifetime of greatly deterred mental ability—retardation. Our mental capabilities are also jeopardized or decreased for life if inadequate nutrition is given us until the age of seven. But the earliest stages of development are also very vital for potentially positive reasons. The very young mind—being more vacant, enthusiastic and uninhibited—takes in information at its fastest rate. It learns because it desires the ability to know how to "have fun" in its new world, not because learning is a forced chore. It also learns rapidly because it hasn't fallen into the trap of "predetermined capability"—it hasn't been conditioned to believe that there is a learning-rate limit and that it can't learn much faster than we slow-minded adults. So, like the bumblebee, it just goes ahead and flies anyway. And, of course, the more amusing the activity, the more the child will delight in consuming the information regarding it, the more the child will forget the "tabu" of learning and proceed to improving his mind. Thus, in the early stages, the three most important contributors to positive development are good prenatal care, adequate nutrition, and entertaining/instructive interaction.

Throughout both the earlier and latter stages, there will always be those who learn at various rates, as there will always be those who better achieve through different teaching methods. This is what makes us individuals. If we as individuals are to be the best that we can be, then a system and curriculum must be administered which allows us to best achieve intellectual growth in our own way at our own rate. An education system that forces us to be lumped together into incompatible groups fosters frustration, envy, and inadequacy due to our impatience concerning being held back by those slower than ourselves, our inability to keep up with those more gifted than ourselves, and the inability of the system to meet our individual needs.

The best education—in all stages of life—revolves around not only consuming and applying the accumulative knowledge of mankind's systems, but also around the level of familiarity and harmony we achieve with our physical being. Our minds and bodies work in conjunction with one another to determine the quantity of data we will be capable of absorbing. Thus, a society must ensure proper nutrition for its citizens not only for good physical health, but also for maximum efficiency of the brain. The brain consists of about ten billion small cells (neurons) having tentacles which bear thousands of protrusions which connect with other protrusions, causing electrochemical impulses (thoughts and information) to be passed back and forth. The protrusions increase as the brain is stimulated or exercised. The brain's left side governs our level of math, logic and analysis, and language; the right side, our imaginative, color, rhythmic/musical, and daydreaming capabilities. There are certain vitamins and physical activities which shall benefit both sides of the brain simultaneously as well as alternately. Methods and procedures must be researched and discovered that will allow this to occur in an ever-increasing fashion.

In the earlier stages of learning, concentration should be focused on the left side for the fact that the young know very little, and information must be consumed before it can be creatively applied. Thus, this time is critical for stocking and enhancing the memory—receiving the fundamentals of education. Rapid word-recognition and comprehension—or, if you prefer, speed-reading—should be the next goal because, the more rapidly and efficiently one reads, the more one can accomplish in later life. In the latter educational stages, sophisticated techniques to sharpen the brain's right side will allow for more advanced application of all acquired knowledge.

The acquisition and successful application of knowledge will greatly vitalize any diligent society. But data has a habit of accumulating very rapidly, and that rapid growth accommodates discoveries in a geometric manner. If one discovery leads to ten more which lead to ten others, one hundred branches of data would have sprung forth just from the original. If individuals were relegated to dwelling in just only a few of these branches, they may yet advance their fields of study. But modern contraptions and systems are forever gaining complexity, with many requiring combinations of many different fields, let alone branches, if they are to adequately perform or expand upon existing capabilities. And the more data a single mind can store regarding various fields, the more masterful of and inventive with the resources the individual can become. For this reason, the educational structure must be improved and updated at a ratio comparable to modern knowledge accumulation. Education must be evolved in generational cycles. To the best of existing knowledge, a particular generation of students would simply get the best education in the most advanced manner that the contemporary societal period had to offer. But also during that time, on through until the next generation, studies would be conducted on the brain and equipment would be amply developed that would increase knowledge-storing capacity as much as possible. The next generation of adults would do the same for their children, and the next for theirs, and so on. Such progress eventually renders the blackboard and chalk as archaic artifacts. But let us never forget: the righteous dictator that is Mother Nature must always be adhered to regarding the accelerated scientific directions we take.

It's only logical that smarter people make a better world. This is especially true when all are taught the reasoning behind the superiority of an egalitarian society and the crucial importance of protecting the natural balance as well as being taught all the cold and logical information and occupational data. When man pilots young minds into this direction, safe and beneficial advancement cannot help but follow. But a societal policy that allows fair access to education is not only uplifting and stimulating, it also establishes a safe intellectual balance—preventing the accumulation of a few technocrats in the face of a mass of technological and fundamental illiterates. Thus, no few humans would acquire a lock on information and strategic resources that would allow them to pirate the freedoms and rights of the masses and force them onto a subjugated road which would eventually lead only to class conflict and animosity.

Societal stability is also perpetuated by the constructive early guidance of the young. "Holistocratic" intelligence is well aware of the dangers of the neglected and idle mind and therefore advocates committing the young mind to good works before it is left to wander. If leadership opens a road leading in a constructive direction, then a person is more likely to follow that road than to build and travel one leading toward a destructive destination. Children initiating and joining disruptive gangs, delinquency, academic apathy—all are basically contributory to the observation that a lack of direction leads to a lack of hope.....especially when a national environment ferments separatism, selfishness, and uncertainty. And, as there must be direction, there must also be a secured pot of gold in front of young eyes—something to shoot for that compels them to invest the time and sweat necessary to accumulate the mental ability to obtain that prize in a legitimate manner. For this, there must be responsible national planning that ensures positive reward for positive action.

Constant, constructive youth activity is an imperative. Much before the collegiate years, the youth must be directed toward fields of interest and compelled—through incentives—to pursue their mastery to the exclusion of all potentially destructive idleness. Along with this, it's also essential that governmental leadership—through strategic planning and foresighted anticipation—selects and offers fields to the youth which shall be in adequate future demand. Because government is the perennial entity regulating societal interaction, its officials would perpetually command the resources pervasive enough to determine approximately the specificity and quantity of goods and services the entire populace needs, wants, and consumes. Concerning the after-school idle time of the youth, society can mollify its potential detriment by establishing programs designed to provide entertaining outlets during the latter hours of the day. During and after the hours of formal education, adult leadership must ensure that the time of the youth is accounted for and is spent beneficially rather than detrimentally toward themselves and others. If not a nurturing parent is available, then the support structure must provide the supervision.

Monetary Management

So far regarding the endeavors of man, we've given him land to control, resources to exploit, a natural covenant of supervision, and an education to make it all jell in the most prosperous and sophisticated of manners. Now comes time to dwell on the ultimate magnetic item which compels the citizenry to wreck their brains utilizing those aforementioned resources in order to obtain it—and which, throughout its entire history, has driven so many soles bonkers in their pursuit of it: MONEY! Yes, its accessibility to the masses must be fairly managed, and I'll elaborate more on that later. But right now, I wish to dwell on its purchasing power.

Imagine an economic environment where the same unit of currency continuously buys the same amount of raw sustenance, the same amount of raw resources, the same basic housing, and basically the same quantity of utilities. Imagine the pricing of these commodities being engineered to allow the buying power of the currency to stretch far and wide in their purchase. With that, imagine that the purchasing of these commodities by the citizenry will also fund the operations of the nation's governmental functions. Now we'll make the picture even more enticing: What if advancing technology continually lowers the cost of producing and purchasing all the aforementioned commodities? Then, with this kind of economic advantage, the general populace would need only a minority of their money for basic necessities, and the nonessentials and luxuries market would bear the potential to reap good profits at all times. Thus, more avenues would be open through which the people could utilize their creativity in the pursuit of wealth.

The most important function of currency is its funding of our survival. The more stable the currency is in this regard, the more amicable the relationship between the citizens in the commercial, employee, and civil sectors. As long as the currency's value regarding necessities is maximized and stabilized, a continuously rising standard of living will bless the populace simply because there would be a solid sustentative (life-sustaining) base from which to build upon. Plus, there would be no life-threatening case for economic discord or systematic rectification. And the prices of nonessentials could rise and fall as market forces dictated, with no real cause for alarm in either case.

However, as nature's imbalances force man to address physical plagues, so do economic ones force him to confront fiscal and budgetary ones. If the sustentative value of the currency is allowed to decline, less consumer money and business capital will be available for the nonessentials market. Also, strife and confrontation enter into the picture: now employees will feel the need to ask for raises—feeling justified because of the escalating cost of living. The nation will be prone to strikes from employees refused wage increases by owners and managers. The human factor comes into play: People will work harder for the same living standard or will sacrifice some of their comfort zone, more resources will have to be consumed to maintain lifestyles, there is less family time, and the resulting psychological stresses surface with increasing intensity.

In a relevant scenario, in a free-market system, too much money on the open market equals inflation—spurring the "overheated economy." Now the headache of economic restructuring will have to be confronted—with adjustments in government spending, interest rates, currency withheld from the market, and by whatever other means necessary. On the other hand, too much money in the hands of the few or too little in those of the masses, then it's recession and even on to depression, triggering the need for programs of assistance, charitable intervention, more stringent crime prevention measures, etc.

Four things to etch in stone regarding a society operating under the ideal platform of socioeconomic-stability/ever-decreasing-cost-of-living:

1) Market forces are acceptable concerning the nonessentials market, but, if a society stresses socioeconomic equity, they are anathema concerning the distribution of necessities to the masses. Allowing market forces to exclude sectors of the populace is OK regarding fancy cars and diamond rings, but it isn't OK regarding food in the stomach or a roof over the head.

2) Seniority rather than inflation (with inflation in actuality being economic instability) should be the principal justification for wage increases in occupations that provide necessities to the populace. Advanced skills command elevated wages, but the cost of living in relation to the value of currency must remain stabilized or minimized, never increasing. Therefore, wages for workers in essential fields must be stabilized. A rise in the standard wages for a particular occupation and skill level indicates poor educational planning—the failure of society to adequately train a future workforce to fill a needed field. And, as always, a shortage in supply generates inflation. Inflation is a detriment that raises living costs and spurs wage conflicts. And, if wage-increases are constantly applied as an attempt to correct wage disparity, this can only perpetuate the detriment of inflation and the need for additional economic corrections.

3) The greatest method a nation can use to raise its living standard is not for it to seek to add more "gold to the pot," rather, it is for it to allow the people to keep more "gold in the pot"— i.e., it should strive to constantly lower the cost of living for its citizens. A nation may be able to fill its pot one period but may have disastrous luck in another. The question is: What did they do with the gold when they had it?

A reduction in living costs not only grants consumers more capital for expenditures, it also serves to minimize the pains of adjustment incurred by the imperfections and deleterious effects inherent in man's socially applied socioeconomic systems. (Errors in the nation's budget management won't hurt the populace as much if the people require less and less to live on.) Occurrences such as natural disasters are less likely to have lingering economic effects as well. The reduction in living costs also usually means that Mother Nature's resources are being more efficiently applied—and that the whole socioeconomic system itself is being efficiently run. Then there is the advantage that an increasingly stronger sustentative base also makes a nation more independent of negative foreign influences.

Also, <u>retirement</u> is a privilege more easily attainable when the citizenry continuously needs less to live on. A few smart economic moves, and more and more people could retire at earlier ages, devoting more of their lives to personal fulfillment rather than to occupational obligations.

By all means, seek to add more gold. But <u>turn</u> that gold into more efficient energy production and consumption, cheaper construction materials, cheaper agricultural processes, and essential services provided for less money.

4) Finally, the quantity of currency in circulation must be substantiated by a market that offers an equivalent amount of products and services in exchange for it (GNP). Currency released in excess of this is monetarily depreciatory—"fiat money" which undermines financial stability and the value of human endeavor. Currency quantity must correspond with formulas centered around the gross national product, with additional amounts being introduced into the system only in the course of an expanding market of goods and services. Unsubstantiated currency is an indication of mismanagement and/or corruption—or of cultural exploitation if the culprit is a foreign power (such as via exploitative high-interest international monetary loans which stimulate the printing of fiat money for repayment).

(Note: Under the semisocialist system, there are three market values determining GNP—governmental, commercial, and global. Governmental market value is production cost plus revenue surcharge, commercial value is production plus profit motive, and global value is whatever the international market offers.)

Now we return to the entity best qualified to manage the application of said GNP formulas—the same entity despised by the oligarchies for its threat to their monopolization of earthly resources: GOVERNMENT. By putting control of the necessities into governmental hands (<u>good</u> governmental hands, mind you), the profit motive would be eliminated, the cost of living would be regulated advantageously toward the populace, and the government itself could be supported by a surcharge added on to the commodities designed to cover its operating costs—the private-profit motive would shift to the national-revenue motive. Through governmental management of the economic formulae, as the production and rendering of feasible products and services increases, more currency would be released unto government and unto banks in a ratio projected to accommodate the increased consumer purchasing-demand, yet that would keep the cost of living stabilized or minimized. The private and public sectors would receive said currency in the form of loans, grants, and payments of other sorts. Competition and consumer demand would weed out the less feasible endeavors from the more feasible ones.

It must also be understood that, as long as the currency remains within the nation, it bears the greatest chance of circulating through all hands of the citizenry—a vigorous economy. In this regard, government is also the perennial entity in preventing international trade from draining a nation's domestic economy—a worldly blow to the heads of the world's exploitative globalist elitist class wanting to play one nation against another (such as by using cheap Third World labor to "dump" cheaply priced products into developed nations to drive down the wages of the higher-paid workers). And, of course, it goes without saying how a strong and stable currency brings a nation high world esteem. Also, by keeping domestic living costs minimal, wages can be maintained at a level that allows a nation to be a very competitive force in the international market. A very strong currency at home and stable one abroad combined with a line of competitively priced products on foreign shelves (barring protectionism) is a formidable economic advantage indeed.

As long as we dwell in bodily form, essentials are absolutely necessary for our upkeep. But life was meant to be more than just food, shelter, and clothing; its greatest purpose is that of discovery, growth, and fulfillment—great goals more easily achieved as we are increasingly liberated from substantial living costs which devour our rewards from labor. Humanity being plagued with high costs of essentials is akin to embarking on a trip to a grand amusement park and expending all money on food and fuel before arriving; the purpose is defeated.....that potential in life is denied. Let us get sustentation fiscally and financially out of the way so that we will have more resources with which to explore the more intriguing and enjoyable aspects of life.

A parting scenario: Family X is an average family of four with an average monthly income of $4,000 and who pays $3,000 each month for necessities (including house payments). They therefore have $1,000 to save and/or spend. The $3,000 sustentative base remains stabilized. Work promotions raise the family income to $5,000, leaving $2,000 for the nonessentials and for savings. Meanwhile, innovations occur which allow resources to be converted less expensively into products, services and utilities—lowering Family X's cost of living to $2,500, thereby giving them $2,500 to spend and save. The extra expendable cash allows more opportunities to be created in the private sector and the complete scenario perpetuates itself, with innovations continually lowering the cost of living and thereby giving the people more money to "have fun" with.

Crime and Punishment

There is no such thing as the perfect man. There is no such thing as the perfect woman. When society begins to adopt a propagated notion that it is indeed infallibly orchestrated, then that is the point at which it is most dangerous to the individual.

There are always going to be impurities and discrepancies in any system of operations that man administers, with so many of them being unpredictable and undetectable. They therefore slip quietly into society's internal structure. Mankind falls prodigiously short of being a master of utopia. Every operation, every systematic setup he plans, is not a permanent sanctified covenant etched in gold; rather, it is a temporary experiment drawn in dust, with the winds of change ready to blow it away when time comes for a new day. As long as man dwells upon the earth, he is a perpetual experiment, never a finished product.

The fact that we must constantly endure our personal struggles between right and wrong is substantial evidence of our incompleteness. A "complete" human society would know that "completely right" can only build and improve while "completely wrong" can only tear apart and destroy. There is so much destruction occurring in the world today—destruction not just by civil violence or by the criminal on the lowly street, but also by the hands of governmental leaders who have decided that their way is the right way and that whosoever renounces their ideals must face the wrath of their "righteous" forces. This can only serve to prove that something BIG is wrong with man as an individual...and as a species. There is definitely something wrong with us when we'd rather face the threat of being blown off the planet in nuclear holocaust than become friends with and help one another. There is definitely something wrong with us when we condone the unlimited accumulation of wealth by the few while allowing the wallowing in inadequacy for so many. And there is something positively most disturbing, and most dangerous, when so many of us cannot comprehend that there is indeed....something wrong.

When civilian society sees the incarcerated staring back through prison bars, the propagandized sentiment to run through the mind is one of: "Righteous justice, rendered and served." But, when considering the historical malfeasance of man, it takes a subjugated and manipulatable mentality to automatically partake in that line of thinking. One must be of the mental level capable of being brainwashed into accepting the fallacy that humanity's systems are omnisciently and infallibly correct—that all forces which dictate our actions have been completely identified and defined, perfectly evaluated, and incorporated flawlessly and righteously into the equation used to establish the society of man and that all soles who violate this "perfect equation" automatically relegate themselves to the detestable level of being "the wrong upon the land." This line of thinking is for those who cater to robotization, not justice...not humanitarianism. Bars and cells in themselves are merely human methods of separation. Human society separates those who perform blatant criminal acts, but it also has been known to confine political prisoners who fought against injustices and known to excessively punish members of a persecuted sector: sometimes it's "more practical" and "socially beneficial" to warehouse than it is to economically empower. As bars and cells are instruments of civilian protection, they can also be symbols of power, oppression, and miscarriages of justice.

There are indeed individuals whose criminal traits are undoubtedly generated purely by their own moral deficiency. But there is another sector of systematic deviants who will be shaped by negative circumstances in detrimental environments. Poverty and physical and psychological abuse are the giants of detrimental environment and circumstance. But, whether or not the individual offender is influenced by these contaminating stimulants, we must learn to hold back our tongues of full rebuke until our feet of full experience tread in their footsteps. When hit with the same set of adversities for as long as they were, who's to say what <u>our</u> reactions might have been? Unless we are very close, how do we know the most intimate of occurrences that shape their daily lives? Also, we have to remember that human bodies themselves are so diverse and different. If we inherited their anatomy, body chemistry, or their genes, would our actions have been better, the same....or worse? But there are deeper, more culpable, answers we must ask ourselves if we are to fairly evaluate the whole picture. In our frantic haste for almighty money, how do we know that the artificial mechanisms and support structures we create don't affect the minds of some individuals more so than we can detect? What about the sex, violence and profanity in our entertainment media? How do we know whether or not the pollutants that we pump into the environment or the preservatives that we allow into our food do not destroy the physical, and thereby the judgmental, capabilities of some more so than others? Look at the whole of society itself: Is there too much poverty, too much racial socioeconomic disparity? How can we know the extent to which, by our own hands, we are all inadvertently contributing to the creation of those whom society has told us to label as "bad"? The answer: We can't. Man cannot possibly identify the extent to which his actions affect the whole of humanity in all ways possible simply because man does not know everything. This is why there is so much research occurring in laboratories; there are yet discoveries upon discoveries to be made. If man were omniscient—and noble in intent as the beneficiaries of this world order wish us to believe—the end result of all of his planning wouldn't be a world in turmoil.....like it so very much is today and has been throughout history.

A society's administrative system is the Master of Operations to which every individual must adhere. Being established by the eternally incomplete hands of mankind, we can never be certain of the human product it is turning out. We therefore must adopt an aura of consultation and curiosity toward the deviant rather than hostility and condemnation if we are to progress toward eliminating crimes against the populace. It's imperative that, throughout legal incarceration and supervision, mankind seeks to consult and learn from the socially deviant—to humanely experiment in order to attempt to discover the root cause of what went wrong. We may find that, if some of their advice is taken and applied, it may prevent many others from following in their footsteps. And the administrative system will be all the better for it, allowing the experiment that is human autonomy to become a little more complete.

Because we are not ultimate beings, we haven't the right to render ultimate judgments. Society hasn't the divine countenance to dictate who does and does not deserve the right to continue life. Until man conquers such malevolent traits as environmental destruction, war, and cultural genocide and exploitation, those individuals who may brutally murder their fellow man aren't the only abominations walking the face of the earth. The standards of those rendering justice must always be above the ones of those being judged. And it's philosophical hypocrisy for man to display his abhorrence of killing by killing. In judgment, vengeful retribution must give way to clear and progressive thinking or man's innate primal furry will overrule his acquired senses. And, in so many cases, our intelligence is the only governor that keeps us from going at each other's throats as well as from impetuously committing tragic mistakes. Cooler heads must prevail, or barbarism is the order of the day. Man must never forget his past and his nature—blood and all. In all truth, if righteous retribution were to descend from the heavens and render capital justice for the deeds done by the all of man, then the ancestral legacy of genocide and slaughter committed by the forefathers of many of those shouting for the noose would place their inherited society under an ethereal judgment of condemnation....."Eye for and eye, tooth for a tooth".....a people for a people.

There are those with the facilities, power and policies who destroy more environment, pillage more money, cause more deaths, and thereby who abolish and traumatize more lives than any individual arsonist, thief, rapist, or murderer ever dared. Yet, these are the same ones whom capitalism sets upon a pedestal.....which is only appropriate since every one of us encompassed by the free-market system is responsible for making these giant monsters—just as we may inadvertently contribute to the making of the little ones.....which only serves to further prove the ineptitude of mankind to master the virtue of infallible judgment. But judgments must be made or anarchy will render the land unmanageable. Somehow, man must balance the factors of deterrence, rehabilitation, and psychological research in his handling of social deviation while also realizing that a hateful criminal justice system often produces a spiteful ex-prisoner who seldom desires to contribute positively to the civilian system that confiscated his freedom.

My final conclusion is that crime and its perpetrators must be inclusively regarded as evidence of humanity's fallibility, not just as abominations which, if vigorously prosecuted, will eliminate all of society's such problems. The practice of simply building prison upon prison is neither deterrently practical nor economically feasible. Studies must be made physically, psychologically, and sociologically or frustration will hinder man's ability to acquire the knowledge to advance through the stages of improving his penal and civil systems. Progress won't be made simply by warehousing or destroying the human evidence of deviance; more of it will simply crop up later on.....to further knock "perfect society" right off its pedestal.

The Humanitarian Outlook

How we view our fellow man is the best yardstick in existence with which to measure our level of spiritual graduation from stage to stage. As we look into the past and compare it to today: Are there more impoverished? More hungry? More illiterates and uneducated? Is there more hate and contempt? Overall, is there more overall misery? Is humanity merging into a more harmonious unit, or is it further splintering into sectors of selfish and malicious intent? If the negatives of the aforementioned traits prevail, then the philosophical modus operandi of mankind is a dismal failure.

The market-based social system is a cold, insensitive structure. Its insidious ability to destroy the peace between fellow men by turning survival into a competition is one self-destructive trait that alone disqualifies it from ever bringing out the better side of man. But another factor surrounding its anatomy is that it must consume—thriving on class cannibalism; someone must be on the bottom so that the gluttonous elite can be sustained at the top. Thus, we end up with oligarchies, laborer subjugation, merge-and-purge, with "throw-away people" not far behind.

The two factors of consumption and competitive survival create an environment of human phobia, fragmentation of the humanitarian base, suspicion, and resentment—not exactly the best traits for a system of human management to foster if it ever hopes to bring mankind together in complete cooperation. Complete cooperation is complete unity. And complete unity is obtainable only when all of humanity views all of its members not as calculated statistics in the game of competitive economics, but as feeling, substantial beings deserving the right of survival, opinion, and prosperity—imperative stabilizing factors if man is to achieve the blessing of peace. The rich will always garner the cream of society's respect; it is those who are economically subordinate who are at the greatest risk of being regarded as manipulatable objects rather than as substantial persons. For this reason, we must adopt a magnanimous policy toward those "lesser" than ourselves.

The capitalistic game's ultimate objective is to create a numerically limited elite ruling a numerically <u>un</u>limited underclass. Along this line, no nation can practice the policy of "benign" neglect regarding the needy and remain secure and vital. When intolerable conditions abound, it is the underclass and excluded who will spark national upheaval. With these points in mind, we come to the understanding that all citizens in all categories must be incorporated into the nation's plans regarding prosperity. If a sector of people aren't included into the mainstream under favorable circumstances <u>initially</u>, they will have to be dealt with by the mainstream under unfavorable circumstances <u>eventually</u>.....whether it is brought about by crime, the spread of disease from neglected health, public dependency, lost productivity, or any other means of impedance that serves to function as a drag on national stability. The conduit to legitimate sustentation and progress must be available to all, giving them little reason to travel in the opposite direction. Exclusivity is a comfortable bed in the present, but a burning house in the future.

One must understand, even though some of us have made it, we can't write off the less lucky. In so many cases, there are individuals in society with talent equal to our own who, through fate alone, are not sitting in the very same prestigious seats that we may now occupy. Who knows? Maybe a step to the left instead of right, a delayed bus, or one hour overslept could have put many of us into the same lowly position. The scrupulous <u>and</u> the unscrupulous are successful in the economic arena. Who knows why fate chose to tap certain individuals on the shoulder with success and others with failure? By the grace of God or fate, our spirits were not placed within their bodies at conception. It is up to our own consciences to ensure that their failure doesn't include deprivation of food, shelter, clothing—all essentials needed to live within a comfortable environment. Maybe, in time, a golden opportunity will allow them <u>their</u> time to shine in society. No one should be punished for being "dumb." No one should be faulted or face livelihood deprivation for inheriting a lower intellect than those possessing a more potent mental ability. There are only so many prestigious social positions to go around, and those who have acquired them should appreciate the fact that they had no more intellectual competition than what they had. Plus more, they should be grateful, not tyrannous, that there are individuals willing to make an honest living catering to their needs. They should take solace in the fact that there is someone to drive a limousine or cab so that they can make that important business meeting, that there's someone to keep their office clean so that they can impress clients, and that there's someone to labor to build what they have designed. The "gifted" should also ensure and take solace in the fact that these individuals are securely provided for so that they may continue rendering their needed services in an atmosphere of contentment. The hands that can feed a kind master are the same ones that can poison a cruel one.

Denying medical care to the under-funded would be an ultimate exhibition of misdirected human priority. What more direct method could society use to tell a person of misfortune they are worthless than to allow their suffering.....even until death? It would be perhaps the highest insult to humanitarianism—as well as a travesty to practicality for the simple fact that treatment rendered promptly and widely prevents epidemics as well as the need for more expensive latter-stage treatment, thusly preserving more resources for all in need. Holding citizens as "financial prisoners" for succumbing to physical conditions beyond their control is also another example of capitalism's cruel and warped fiscal policies when practiced by nations possessing adequate wealth to care for the health of their citizenry. The money is there; before it gets released into society's dog-eat-dog economic circulatory system in its entirety, let us preserve the portions necessary to treat the sick—just as they should be preserved to educate the future generations for society's needed occupations. No one should escape their sickbed and be faced with the awesome task of competing in a vicious economic game in a strenuous effort to latch onto currency—that appears to be more precious than themselves—for the purpose of paying for their spared lives. There is one other matter of importance: As we can never precisely determine the exact extent to which our combined activities affect human behavior, so can we never exactly determine the actual amount to which we all contribute to the deterioration of individualistic health. The chemicals and emissions that we all support circulate through the water, the atmosphere, and the land and unavoidably come into contact with our bodies. (And also again, what about the preservatives and artificial ingredients we allow into our foods?) The overwhelming majority of individual soles have no choice as to the chemical allowances society as a whole permits to be emitted into the environment or as to how he or she will be adversely affected. The individual must trust society to decide these things.....and society is everybody. Thus, in minimal words, this makes us all "liable" to one another.

Though money has probably been history's most effective catalyst for corruption, it is still vested with the power to facilitate the distribution of society's needs and wants. Its abundance and scarcity determine the extent and quality of opportunity that we are privileged to encounter. And since we all have needs and wants, we all must have access to economic opportunity to a tolerable degree. It would be well and fine if there existed an unlimited supply of currency which retained a perpetual value. But, since this isn't the case, and since currency is directly connected to a nation's prosperity, then there must be limits and safety guards in place to keep the have-mores from obtaining too much and the have-lessers from receiving too little. The amount of currency available for a nation's healthy economic circulation is limited to the amount of goods, resources, and services that the nation possesses which can support the currency's value. The more/less currency in circulation, the higher/lower the price of these commodities. "Limited" means that society cannot allow an infinite amount of currency to fall into the hands of the few without depriving others. Money has been canonized and engineered to be the lifeblood of free-market societies; virtually nothing significant can be accomplished without it. A well-fed organism accomplishes much; a malnourished one withers away to disease and idleness. The heart cannot keep all the blood to itself, nor can the brain. It must circulate throughout the entire body if the body is to remain well, vital, and alive. Since man has made individuals totally dependent upon the economic circulatory system, he must have the heart and brain to realize that the attitude and capability of his fellow men can be elevated only when adequate economic lifeblood is allowed to circulate throughout the entire body of the masses. If not, then the body will cannibalize itself—amputating its own limbs with corruption, crime, and separatism. The strength of a nation is not the abundance possessed by its elite, but the status endured by its whole.

Population Control

You are to be sealed within a chamber for one day, wherein there is adequate oxygen to sustain one individual comfortably for twenty-four hours and ample space available to shift the body through various comforting positions. You breathe and move normally and without reservation. Later, another individual is added. Now you must breathe more conservatively and move with more constraint, being careful to conserve the life-sustaining gas and to allow space for the other person. Two more are added. Now you must time yourself to breathe at an even less capacity and to comfort your body in one-fourth the space. At this stage, the absence of any individual would be considered a great blessing. If more are added than can be compensated for by the human respiratory system, suffocation is the result, and the presence of human company has become a deadly threat to one's existence.

The earth—the chamber within which we are sealed—is only so big. Though its size is viewed in cosmic proportions, its 8,000-mile diameter provides a finite infrastructure which can facilitate just enough of a support system to sustain only so much human and subhuman life. The world we live in is matter, and matter is neither created nor destroyed, merely rearranged. The human body is matter; though we regard it in anthropocentric terms as a sacred composition of supreme substantiality, it's still composed of worldly "stuff." While man dwells on this planet, the life-support matter is rearranged into human matter, with the support matter decreasing as the human matter is increasing. This is all bearable to the individual as long as survival and living space are somewhat accessible. However, allow the support base and comfort zone to become seriously limited, then people begin to regard one another as "inconveniences." If the population growth is left unchecked, this will progress to a game of "musical chairs," with the chairs as the support base and the welfare of the people as the players. At this point, human beings become things. They become organic obstacles to overcome for survival and expendable tools for the affluent to exploit—competitors and pawns in the competition for sustentative resources in the realm of an ever-contaminated environment. Human beings will fight for survival—if necessary, by any means available. When the human matter has outstripped the life-support matter to a desperate extent, there is one tragic and barbarous recourse—human matter consuming human matter—cannibalism.....the ultimate competition. A horror which has already occurred multiple times past in recorded history.

The bottom line: If we don't control population growth ourselves, then all the converging forces of nature will. If nature does so, she will implement it with absolutely no apologies as far as severity and with little consideration of comfort or of "human superiority." If we become wise and take it upon ourselves, there will be pains of philosophical conflict, physical preparation, and of routine procedures, but they will be planned for and thereby will be more bearably predictable and tenable. One outcome illustrates man's immaturity, fragmentation, and environmental complacency to such an extent that his natural mother must whip him down with misery, deficiency, and ecological disaster. The other outcome shows man's noble growth—his awakening to the responsibility of being caretaker of this borrowed planet and protector of the needs of future human life, an outcome where generation praises generation for engineering the conditions for quality life.....unlike the opposite one where generation blames generation for the causing of life's deficiencies and hardships.

So far, I've discussed the sunny side of my preferred form of human administration: equal access to life-sustaining land, resources, and to education; cooperation between men; the elevation of societal capabilities—the endearing side of human autonomy. But now comes time to delve into the black waters of forced human-behavioral control. Population control is the painful side of semisocialism—as it would be in any governmental system which adopts it. It is so because, whether voluntarily heeded or ruthlessly enforced, it must be implemented in order to avoid a complete breakdown in the semisocialist system. Overpopulation is the principal natural element that could overload and short-circuit the system's ability to provide adequate sustentative capabilities for all citizens. And the stabilizing factor of individual-worth being substantiated by equal-land control would continually depreciate into nothingness.

How important is population control? Important enough to where a powerful official department should be established solely for its implementation. Important enough to where individual compliance is not choice, is not duty, but is the law. Important enough to where one's autonomy is thrown completely out the window if found hostile to its enforcement. It is one imperative that justifies invading homes and forcing over-productive parents into clinics for sterilization. It's so essential, that it warrants man engineering his entire societal setup around its guidelines—setting a limit on the amount of land that can be humanly exploited, preserving a permanent amount of land for the accommodation of a safe and strong ecological cycle, and setting a family-size limit which continuously decreases in number as the population approaches its designated maximum. It justifies the establishment of economic incentives that reward the compliers and penalize the violators, forcing those who produce an excessive number of offspring to bear more of the economic burden of providing for their welfare and granting the compliers better access to all systematic opportunities leading to success. Early-term abortion would certainly be an allowable form of population control, but its instigation would be completely left to the decision of the parents, never to that of governmental force.

The universal factors concerning overpopulation must be acknowledged and managed in man's journey toward a stable societal foundation. First, we must understand that poverty and idleness foster heavy procreation while wealth and industriousness tend to produce less. The poor are more inclined to procreate more abundantly, with their offspring bringing them a sense of importance as well as giving them someone with whom to share mutual affection. (Of course we have the other socioeconomic factors, such as lack of birth control, the availability of sex in crowded slums, and some welfare systems that may compensate procreation.) In some cultures, children provide security in the form of labor for agrarian families. Some cultures use procreation as a political weapon; some promote it for assurance of future hegemonic control. Some portions of the affluent bear the greater tendency to view children as a nuisance—an unwanted diversion from their "more productive" endeavors. Also, a successful working couple—or single individual—in industrial societies has less time and energy for passionate encounters. Sex that is practiced by the affluent bears the greater possibility of being complimented with birth control and abortion procurement.....the wealthy woman wanting to retain her "social" anatomical figure or, if unwed, to garner the high social esteem that comes with having no illegitimate children. To the poor, sex serves as a pleasure device as with the other classes, but it also tragically serves as a means of escape from harsh environmental realities. They are less likely to practice birth control or fetal termination. The effects of the poor/wealthy dichotomous procreative sentiment can be witnessed in the variations in population density in the Third and industrial worlds.

Secondly, we must never underestimate the importance of land management in relation to civil harmony. Once heavy population is rampant and in concentration in the poorer areas, the close proximity of human bodies ferments close and frequent carnal temptation. Also, unemployment leaves much idle time for sexual encounters. The effect of having an excess of individuals territorially concentrated not only creates a mass of vulnerable servants for the rich, it also fosters a climate of incompassion and apathy among fellow territorial members. People in this afflicted environment are less likely to care for one another, and the slam-bam-thank-you-ma'am sentiment prevails. (Let us also take notice of the geometric transmission of diseases in relation to population density—the sexual as well as the nonsexual.) Peers become transformed into life-threatening competitors, with the abundance of their numbers—their "detrimental presence"— spurring a rise in the cost of the very land upon which everyone stands. "Five people in a one-room shack" is a sign of degeneration, not progress. Cities become the devil's playground and criminal factory. Man's spirit wasn't meant to be tormented with constant, and often undesired, human contact. Nor was it meant to be sardine(d) into crowded structures. The tranquilizing effect of land ownership is that it allows one to have one's space to be oneself—to be _free_. Land management must be arranged in such a manner that it habilitates adequate human separation.....and thereby preserves the peace between men. The quality of life that adequate living space can bring makes the struggle for peace worth striving for.

Finally, we must become more aware of the responsibilities of man's mental superiority in regard to the preservation of nature. Man owes it to nature to avoid all ecological epicenters when constructing residential areas or building facilities of significant environmental impact. It's simple: He can create artificial support systems; the lower species cannot. Subhuman creatures must dwell near their sustenance. As said, nature possesses biological characteristics that man may never completely understand; therefore, as much of nature that can be preserved <u>must</u> be preserved at all costs. As he further progresses technologically, man must increase his efforts to withdraw from the aforementioned epicenters, creating wildlife reservation gaps never to be publicly inhabited by the general populace. A sparse dispersal of humanity into the less vital areas—a patch here, a patch there—is not only ecologically beneficial in that it allows the gaps to subsist, it also creates the smaller-community familiarity which soothes residential interaction. Man's ability to construct structures for living, for shading, to produce artificial materials, to harvest natural energy-producing forces, and to produce indoor temperature control devices present him with a number of options regarding climates and land conditions to choose from. The development of advanced farming techniques will further liberate humanity from the need to inhabit vital land space. The advantage of piping allows man to live any distance from all surface-water epicenters such as lakes, ponds, and rivers; fish farms could be established to produce aqua food artificially. Evolving landscaping abilities could mollify the denaturalizing effects of man's synthetic structures through the use of applications such as artificially sustained vegetation and man-made ponds—insurances that nature's pristine countenance would never be dominated by man-made artificiality to the point that the minds and spirits of the populace would be far removed from the ecological covenant. As long as he maintains a reasonable population limit, man will always command options as to how his civilization will be incorporated into Earth's cycles. Overpopulation—whether regional, national, or global—forces humanity to maintain a pervasive presence upon the earth's surface, causing it to fill in the epicentral gaps and "bump into" nature, which, as we know, often leads to extinction and other disastrous ecological results. Even though much of the world has already been developed, future development could implement this epicentral withdrawal—as could existing cities be disassembled and dispersed more sparsely and ecologically. There must be incentives to maintain an adequate domestic population, but there also must be disincentives against practicing excessive procreation. Too many people, and society succumbs to destitution, indifference, and conflict; too few, and nations crumble and fall. Population regulation must be as mandatory and as mechanically performed as the balancing of a national budget....rendering absolutely no leniency toward over-productive citizens. Maintaining the ideal level is the challenge that no nation can fail to pursue. Societal stability hangs in the balance.

It is my opinion that one of the greatest services that humanity could perform for this planet would be to depopulate through attrition while simultaneously rectifying problems and reshaping human priorities—though this is a prodigiously improbable scenario, I know....and "inconvenient to the world's social security systems." In brief: What the world needs now are <u>solutions</u>, not an increase in human life. More soles being born into a pressure-cooker world than can be comfortably accommodated can only serve to heap burden upon recurring burden, which the malevolent side of man consistently brings upon itself. Now is the time for man to come to grips with the reality of numbers and the challenge of incorporating them into a benevolent scheme that offers greater purpose and opportunity for all existing and future human life that is to dwell upon this planet.

(Population Statistics—from Overpopulation.org)

World population growth: 1915: 1.8 billion | 1967: 3.5 billion | 2006: 6.5 billion | 2011: 7.0 billion. October 2006—U.S. Census Bureau.

The normal rate of extinction is about one in a million species per year. The extinction rate today is between 100 to 10,000 times that.—Postcarbon Institute 2010.

The loss of biodiversity through deforestation alone will cost the global economy up to US $4.5 trillion each year - $650 for every person on the planet. The Economics of Ecosystems and Biodiversity.—(TEEB) project, 2010. Half a billion people live in water-stressed or water-scarce countries, and by 2025 that number will grow to three billion. In the last 50 years, cropland has been reduced by 13% and pasture by 4%.—U.N., June 2005.

If fertility remained at current levels, the population would reach the absurd figure of 296 billion in just 150 years. Even if it dropped to 2.5 children per woman and then stopped falling, the population would still reach 28 billion.—Bill McKibben, May 1998 - Atlantic Monthly.

The world's best-kept little secret: family planning saves lives, boosts economic growth, and makes for a safer world. Suzanne Ehlers, President and CEO of Population Action International.

Man's Peaceful Purpose

What are we here for? Were our corporeal and spiritual forms engineered by a higher being, nature, or by some other force unfathomable to the human mind? Why is it that we are the only earthly creatures that can build and use sophisticated tools? That can contemplate and express thoughts in such complex terms? These tantalizing quandaries have infatuated mankind for its entire linguistic history. The fact that we harbor these curiosities serves to illustrate one insatiable yearning—to desire to obtain a higher knowledge of the cosmic realities of the universe, leading to our promotion to a higher calling.

The most evocative question—"Is this all that life's about?"—is the predominant force which drives us to ponder the possibility of a higher calling. So far, the unfulfilling occupation of man has been a spiritually depreciating one that has been dominated by the struggle for survival, reproduction, and materialistic acquisition. The drudgery and seemingly futile repetitiveness of these activities has led many of us to wonder, "Is this all there is? Where are we going? How will we know when we've arrived?" These provocative questions permeate our conscience not only because of our intrinsic curiosity, but also because there's something vital missing in the annals of humanity. And that "something" is a plan of unity through which all individuals can work in order to reach the objective of a higher calling—of human elevation leading to evolution.

Man lives by sight, not by faith. I'm not saying it <u>should</u> be this way; I'm just stating the fact that it <u>is </u>this way. If man lived by faith, then all activity and outcome would be predictable through his adherence to religious doctrine. Instead, our actions are motivated by the solid concreteness of this world and how we can manipulate that which is before our eyes to our greatest advantage. Thus, those who say that we should "leave everything up to God" are, in actuality, impediments (albeit unintentionally) to man's chances of obtaining unity through direct human action. This is due to the fact that man is hypocritical religiously, is agnostic, is nonreligious—and who's to say whose god is the <u>real</u> god? But the spirit of the gods has basically been consistent—one of constructiveness incorporated with morality, along with a strict discipline to work through the established laws of nature. Also, there is another vital tendency—the tendency that God cares for humanity <u>through</u> humanity; the work is executed by the minds, muscles, and internal spirits of human beings. There's no obvious magical force that descends from the heavens to remove the mountains from the path of human endeavor. A belief in world salvation through the Almighty is fine, but it is absolutely no excuse for standing idle in a world full of injustice and misery.

If we are ever to emulate an aura of "godliness"—to evolve to a higher calling as a species—we must develop the ability within ourselves to utilize this concrete world to the greatest advantage of all life which exists upon it. We must implement this process ourselves if sight-guided man is to witness any encouraging signs that humanity is gaining more sanctity and that therefore foster in him a desire to secede from the ranks of the war mongers and exploiters of his fellow men. Rampant fragmentation has confused the minds of humanity. Frustration, and insensitivity toward the needs of others, are dominant results of our hostility toward our human brothers and sisters. But they are also the result of a lack of direction—the lack of a cohesive aspiration that would ingratiate man to work with man to develop this world as a collective whole. Mankind will achieve its greatest progress when all work in total unison to accomplish objective after objective. And this is achievable only through the establishment and adoption of one essential ingredient—a plan.

A benevolent plan—showing where we are going and how we will get there—would serve as the powerful magnet which draws humanity together in creative unison, which renders a definite purpose to mankind's existence. "Unity" means that the survival of all is precious and of paramount importance to all. And when survival is better guaranteed, it takes much of the anxiety out of living, and peace is the result—peace through which the mind can better contemplate and pursue the process of human advancement.....for all humans desiring to advance. When we all have a general idea of "where we are going" and "what we must do to get there," then we as individuals could incorporate ourselves into the structural blueprint in any manner that suits our abilities—whether the field is science, health, construction, societal improvement and advancement, etc.—continuously expanding the knowledge and facilitative base for everyone.

Humanity is forever a singular metamorphic organism, constantly initiating and enduring philosophical and technological mutations. Though many of us view ourselves as individualistic entities autonomously directed or superiorly endowed, we are all inevitably connected. Superiority—"racial superiority"—is merely a fleeting gift provided for a time by nature in order to allow human prosperity and resource conservation to coexist at a common time, with those who progress being the consumers and those remaining more primitive functioning as the conservationists. The only superior thing on Earth is nature's ability to impose change—changes in nature, changes in human society. So many civilizations have risen and fallen all over the world. And, along the way, innumerable contributions were borrowed and passed on. For this reason, no race, color, creed, sex or ideological sector has a right to impose their methodology on others as an eternally superior doctrine. All over Earth, there is evidence exposed and documented exhibiting human triumphs and failures, evidence that is waiting to be studied and incorporated by those with the open minds seeking societal amelioration. The entire human race owes it to itself to take a little bit of this, a little bit of that—small portions of everyone's creativity. Those who vehemently espouse separation inescapably owe something back to that remaining sector who helped create the very advantages which their xenophobic selves wish to "hoard up" and "run away" with. They have forgotten where they come from. Just maybe, if their isolationist leaders were stripped of these intercultural gifts, their converging followers wouldn't like what they were running to. As incest leads to retardation, isolation leads to ignorance. Those who promote unity are the truly evolved of the world, for they long to embrace eclectic creativity which has been spurred by natural forces in all the varied planetary regions.

The roots of humanity's tree will indomitably exist, though the civilized fruit it bears will bloom, ripen, and fall to the ground to deteriorate after their reigns have run their course. The common origin of mankind will inevitably draw it closer together into contact; the "organism" interacts whether or not its subordinate racial organs plan its occurrence. As natural matter returns to its original form—fetus to animal to dust, seed to plant to soil, rock to magma—so, too, does modern man feel drawn toward primitive man. Colonialistic exploitation of the world's natives and transplants was permeated with interracial sexual encounters, not just to inject "good blood" into the debased populace, but also because of the availability of "savage," raw sex, uninhibited by the need for sophisticated romance or polite civil conduct. Getting away to a passive island, fantasizing about that untamed sexual encounter, such things as practicing nudity or roughing it in the wild—all are indicative of a need to return to the primitive setting. This is, in a sense, a way of "going back home," gaining independence from civilization and "starting over"—a way of escaping from the hectic direction man has taken.....escaping to the original perfections of timeless nature and from the nascent imperfections of modern man. It is a romantic aura of an easier life, the elements of which one could better comprehend and master. After all, should all of modern civilization collapse, these are the timeless skills that will sustain the survivors.

As opposites attract (such as modern man to primitive man), varying cultures will attract one another—if not for cerebral, egoistical, pleasurable, or economic purposes, then for the purpose of quenching some other inconspicuous or unfathomable thirst which their native society has been unable to. If we are to be drawn together, let us be drawn together by a plan—a plan which will render us as xenophiles rather than xenophobic, a plan which would make all of Earth a stable place to dwell. Strong societies are maintained by an ideological homogenization, not a racial one. Multiple conflicts and expulsions have occurred intra-racially. Those who believe in the ideology of peace and unity must congregate and work in cooperation in the face of those who do not—if necessary, even taking such steps as establishing intercultural colonies which work together to further the collective progression of man. These settlements could serve as the world's model and as the spearhead in humanity's plan of advancement.

The unifying plan could also encompass the establishment of a worldwide constitution advocating equitable distribution of the resources, equal justice for all, and mutual sustentation. Such benefits listed would be fair worldwide resource distribution, economic aid and development, all needed emergency relief, and mutual technological advancement. The requirements would be that all participating nations practice ecological husbandry, socioeconomic equity, population control, and that they grant their citizens fair human rights never to be violated. Though some world regions are blessed with industrial resources more so than others, a worldwide equitable distribution initiative would allow the all of man to participate in the advancement and amelioration of human life: Plagues could be discovered and tended to in limited locales long before they branch out and afflict the whole of humanity, and more minds blessed with scientific facilities equals more potential to develop and harvest the benefits of such fields as superconductivity and nuclear fusion.

Any plan must have an ultimate objective, and the greatest ultimate goal that sight-guided man can possibly achieve is supreme evolution (some may say "becoming one with God")—complete cosmic awareness to a point where virtually all mysteries of the universe are open to him. This can occur only when the mind of man is so advanced that it can consume and manipulate seemingly infinite knowledge. So, now we must return to the "semisocialist" principles of education which were priorly stated—where an existing generation labored to evolve the mental capacity of the next generation, and so on, and so on. This educational process, coupled with its ultimate goal, bears the great intrinsic benefit of geometric progression for man. As successive generations are fed increasingly sophisticated data, it will geometrically accelerate the rate at which better homes will be built, better food grown, better health maintained—a more comfortable and palatable standard of living for humanity in general. Not a very bad advantage to reap while pursuing the day when we may leave this earth and meet up with the real god.....who may be calling us to come home.

Final Note & Summary:

The natural order: Higher calling, nature, man. When either of these is moved out of place, mankind's guidance and motivations become misplaced. Man needs a higher calling—or God—for purpose, giving him something to strive for, to make life universally worthwhile.....a shining star at the end of his endeavor to elevate. Nature: the provider of sustentation, and the ecological balance which warns man when his steps toward progression have gone awry and which rewards him with the most powerful and purest of conquests when all is well and good. And man himself is the object of affection, the "grand experiment" vested with the greatest potential to discover the ultimate meaning of sentient existence.

Government's domain: environmental preservation, equitable sustentation, human rights, individual prosperity. Since nature is the base of life, its protection and preservation must be stringently regulated and maintained for all existing and future generations; this includes strict limitations on population growth so that ecological boundaries will never be transgressed. Unless the life-sustaining resources of nature are made accessible to the masses, then the masses, as well as society itself, could not exist. It is therefore essential that no few hands are legally allowed to have so much that so many other hands have so little—in the name of survival, in the name of peace, regarding human liberty. The role of government is to ensure that individual actions are not harmful to the environment, to others, or in violation of secular law. Here, morality isn't the issue.....rights are. And that which legal-aged consenters choose to do by themselves or with others is to be left totally up to their own accord, provided that reasonable discretion is practiced where necessary in consideration of those who would be reasonably offended if such practices were conducted in an unrestricted manner in full public view. Man can legislate safety to better ensure civil protection, but he cannot legislate morality without treading into dangerous and murky grounds which jeopardize individual freedoms all should possess and without letting the personal sentiment of some dictate the legal rights of others. Prosperity is the personal goal which motivates individual effort and creativity and which thereby functions as the foremost impetus in human advancement. The rate at which a society is elevated through discovery and advancement and approaches monetary equilibrium is directly tied to the extent to which all citizens are allowed access to systematic facilities in order to exploit them to their most capable advantage. It is idleness—when mixed with poverty and lack of opportunity—which can erode the better attitude and the more productive side of man. Multiple channels to success for all must be maintained by regulation so that all will desire to contribute to the system which sustains and caters to their welfare. If not, then turmoil will flow through the land in exploitation, poverty, frustration, stress, animosity, and rebellion.

How much we choose to interact with and attempt to shape the world is totally left up to us as individuals. But there is a depressingly ominous albatross which flies over the head of every conscious man, woman, and child in this world. Whether one wishes to live within the original harmonies of nature or one desires to dangle in the melodies of mechanisms and technological wonders in an attempt to better master nature's forces and resources, one fact is for certain: When it comes down to conflict and battle, the progressionists always defeat the nonprogressionists. For this reason, any society which wishes to remain respected, vital—and above all, free—must master the higher technological studies on a better or equal basis compared to all others who have done so in the world. It's a shame that the threat of death, destruction, and dominance should set the tone for humanity's endeavors instead of peaceful autonomous impulse serving as the catalyst. It's a shame, and it's so unfair to those who would have chosen otherwise. It's such a travesty that the beasts of the world make the lambs of the world yearn to turn their hunting spears into nuclear missiles in order to remain free in this world; so unfair that the oppressed status of so many is perpetuated by the foreign greed of so many. Fate chose to give some of us so much more and the rest of us so much less. But, then, life is unfair in so many of the cards it deals us. We can only use our humanitarian intelligence to fathom the things that must be equitably obtainable by all and our administrative intelligence to engineer and manage the process which will allow this to occur and endure.

Therefore, with all said, I proclaim that, because man.....

.....is imperfect and aggressive by nature

.....is progressive, passive, and avaricious

.....has inalienable rights to life-sustaining necessities

.....has a right to prosper by merit

.....and must protect his society from outside aggression.....

.....a semisocialist system would be the form of humanly applied government harboring the greatest potential to progressively and harmoniously manage these traits.

Chapter 2

PROPOSED GOVERNMENTAL SETUP

The various ingredients necessary for civilized human existence must be regulated according to content, supply, and the needs of the societal population. The following is my proposal describing a basic setup which will allow any particular nation blessed with the adequate resources to manage these ingredients governmentally and economically according to semisocialism. Understand, this is by no means to insinuate that my way is the only way. The semisocialist system will always be open to receiving your submissions for governmental platforms that you have designed to lead to evolutionary progression—and your better ideas will be incorporated.

(Note: All heads of all governmental offices will be elected for <u>life</u>, removable only upon retirement, resignation, incompetency, corruption, and/or adequate public discourse.)

Government (Listing)

Constitution

National Directive Conglomerate (NDC)

Legislative Branch
House of Provincial Senators
NDC Printing Office
TBA (Treasury, Budget, and Accounting Office)

Executive Branch
President
Presidential Staff
Presidential Offices

(Executive Departments)
Department of Defense
  World Weapons Design and Manufacturing Agency
Department of Education
Department of Health and Safety
Department of the Interior
Department of Land Management
Department of Law Enforcement
Department of Livelihood
Department of Population Control
  National Census Agency
  Bureau of Immigration and Naturalization
Department of Resource Management
Department of Seniority
Department of State

Department of Sustenance
Department of Transportation
Department of Utilities
Treasury Department
  Executive Accounting Office

National Reserve
Director
Director's Staff

(National Monetary Offices)
Office of Monetary Management
Banking Management and Investment Office
NDC Budgeting Office
OCC Budgeting Office
Monetary and Postal Printing Office
National Vault
TBA Office

(National Reserve's Bureau of Distribution)
National Banking System
Division of Sustenance Distribution
Division of Resource Distribution
Division of Utilities Collection
Division of Rent Collection
Division of Transportation Collection
Division of Penalties Collection
National Postal Service

Official Citizens' Conglomerate (OCC)

Council of the People

(Congregational Branch)
House of Provincial Councillors:
Provincial Councillors
Council's Printing Office
TBA Office

(Interactive Branch)
Prime Councillor
Prime Councillor's Staff

Prime Councillor's Offices of Policy:
Office of Human Relations
Office of Human Advancement
  Board of Holistic Incorporators
Office of Economic Advancement
Office of Legal Incorporation
Office of Domestic Defense

TBA Office

Prime Councillor's Interactive Divisions:
Division of Patents, Trademarks, and Copyrights
Research and Development Agency
Division of Behavioral Sciences
Division of Education Advancement
Agency for Space Exploration
Library of Human Advancement
Master Documented Program
Division of Program Coordination
Division of Child Supervision
Collective Earth Organization

Prime Councillor's Military Agencies:
National Guard
Domestic Weapons Agency
Agency for Disaster Relief

Conglomerate of Commercial and Industrial Operations (CCIO)
Director
Director's Staff
Executive Board of Advisors

(Divisions of Industry and Commerce)
Office of Product Selection
Division of Research and Development
Office of Facilities Allotment
Office of Resource Management
Division of Commercial Production
Division of Commercial Sustenance Production
Office of Quality Control
Product Marketing Agency
Citizens' Advertising Agency
Division of Civil and Governmental Production
Office of Civil and Governmental Design
Office of Industrial Design
Office of Foreign Design
International Trade Agency
TBA Office

Official Citizens' Independent Agencies
Office of Economic Balance (plus Foreign Goods Regulatory Office)
National Agency of Investigation
Commission of Election and Recall
Land Allotment Commission
Resource Allotment Commission
Sustenance Allotment Commission

Product Inspection Agency
Arts, Media, and Entertainment Regulatory Commission
Citizens' Media Network

National Judiciary System
Supreme Court of Governmental Affairs
Supreme Court of Civil and Criminal Affairs
Judicial Commissioners
Commissioners of Trial Jurors
Commissioners of Panel Members
All other needed, lower courts.

CONSTITUTION

The Constitution shall serve as the official writ which defines the nation's ideological doctrines, with the doctrines being based upon the right of all to live and prosper to the extent which a balanced ecological system and individual human rights will allow. It shall stress the right of all to the essentials necessary for the sustentation of life, the right of all to be heard who have a constructive message, and the right of all to be protected from exploitation and from infringement upon their human rights.

It shall list the guidelines and define the boundaries to which the nation must adhere regarding military action and regarding an included article stating that the military industrial complex will never overtake the nonmilitary one to the point of domestic decline unless hostile forces are an overwhelming threat to national security.

It shall lay the guidelines for establishing the minimum wage (or, if you prefer, the "living wage") and shall also stipulate that governmental spending shall never create a suffocating economic environment for citizens who seek private prosperity in a fair and noble manner.

Finally, the nation's official writ shall set a population limit, with the intent being that said limit shall never be increased. (Since the standard of living can be improved only when resources become more accessible, a burgeoning population can only serve to increasingly deplete that accessibility, thusly diluting the citizens' ability to experience life at its fullest. A deteriorating lifestyle is a most ardent enemy of any nation's security.)

NATIONAL DIRECTIVE CONGLOMERATE
(Note: In this proposal, the nomenclature is geared toward provinces.)

The National Directive Conglomerate (NDC) will serve as the director, regulator, manager, operator, and protector of the basic infrastructure. Its functions will include upholding the Constitution; establishing, enforcing, and amending the laws and regulations necessary to efficaciously manage the citizenry; protecting the environment; distributing the natural and economic resources both essentially and progressively; collecting the revenue; handling foreign affairs; and militarily protecting the nation from foreign hostility. Basically, it will handle the heavy, daily routines of managing the nation's essential affairs.

Legislative Branch

House of Provincial Senators— elected by their individual provinces. House shall function as a one-party system, with individual ideology serving as the sole method of distinction between members. Senators shall serve as the people's official voice in government and shall establish, debate, and amend laws, regulations, and policies and shall also contribute to the determination of national direction. They must be consulted by the president regarding all significant decisions, will have mandatory access to reports from the president's subordinate executives, and will require a 60% vote to overrule the president or to pass actions. The House shall also have the right to petition the Supreme Court of Governmental Affairs regarding any National Reserve actions that it feels would be significantly detrimental to national affairs. The Chief Senator (elected by the House) shall lead all activity, keep order at sessions, head up the mandatory House reports, and shall appoint the heads to the NDC Printing Office and the TBA Office. By law, only the president, provincial councillors, and the prime councillor (representatives of the general citizenry and not of special interests) shall have direct lobbying access to the legislature.

NDC Printing Office— will produce all NDC printings.

Treasury, Budget and Accounting Office (TBA Office)— shall store and keep track of funds allotted for and expended on senatorial salaries, on the upkeep of legislative operations, and on official activities. Budgeting shall file the annual report for the legislature's projected operating costs (to be determined by all House members) for the upcoming year in order to obtain those funds from the National Reserve. Accounting shall file the annual report on legislative spending to the Reserve.

Executive Branch

President— shall appoint and supervise all heads of the executive branch, will maintain the national infrastructure and operate it as efficiently as possible, shall conduct foreign affairs, shall initiate military action regarding foreign affairs.

Presidential Staff— shall assist the president in dealing with government officials and with the public.

Presidential Offices— shall consist of offices headed by experts in various fields who shall help the president shape policies in the diverse areas of presidential responsibility.

(Executive Departments)

Department of Defense— will execute all military operations geared toward nullifying foreign hostility which threatens national security.

   World Weapons Design and Manufacturing Agency— shall design and manufacture all weaponry used in foreign military affairs.

Department of Education— will provide free public education at all levels while using the most advanced teaching methods. Will supervise the construction of learning institutions. Shall keep track of the amount of professionals in all categories which the nation will need in the diversified future workforce and will provide free collegiate and technical education geared toward filling that future workforce.

Department of Health and Safety— shall ensure every citizen of adequate health care, will supervise the construction of medical facilities, and will enforce national safety standards.

Department of the Interior— will enforce the protection of the environment and manage its maintenance.

Department of Land Management— will manage the daily routines of distributing equal land control to the citizenry, overseeing and aiding in land dealings, maintaining excess land for public or governmental usage, and putting land up for vote regarding public or private usage.

Department of Law Enforcement— will control and operate the nation's police force, will operate the nation's prisons and supervise their construction, and will operate programs of deterrence.

Department of Livelihood— will ensure every citizen of a living place, will initiate and supervise the construction of affordable housing, will ensure all citizens of sustentative necessities and of employment, shall enforce job truancy on all who depend upon the government for livelihood supervision, and shall ensure livelihood security for the disabled.

Department of Population Control— will take all necessary steps to prevent the population from exceeding the constitutional limit. Shall enforce laws concerning overpopulation.

National Census Agency— shall keep a count of all citizens. Shall record and store all significant national citizenry statistics affecting livelihood. Shall function as the indicator of the high or low prosperity level of the various individual citizens, with the information being used to stimulate their economic elevation. Shall function as the indicator of when steps should be enacted to restrict population growth. The agency will also listen to the various opinions of the people and record them in the form of polls, suggestions, and complaints.

Bureau of Immigration and Naturalization— self-explanatory.

Department of Resource Management— will extract raw resources from nature at an ecologically balanced rate and deposit them at the National Reserve. Will also handle the burdens of internationally trading the nation's abundant resources for the ones in which it is deficient.

Department of Seniority— will operate, maintain, manage, and distribute all facilities and necessities geared toward maintaining the livelihood of all elderly in need of aid. Shall distribute subsistence payments—Seniors' Retirement Fund—to retired or elderly seniors.

Department of State— shall handle its normal duties of dealing with global affairs, representatives, and foreign visitors. Shall issue all passports and visas.

Department of Sustenance— will raise and/or store all of the nation's crops and livestock which shall be used by the government, sold to the civilian sector, or traded on the international market. Will deposit sustenance at the National Reserve. Will handle the routines of international trade. Will also gather water from excess supplies and from heavy rains and floods and store it in large tanks nationwide for use in time of droughts—especially for use in agriculture.

Department of Transportation— shall control and operate the nation's essential domestic and international public transportation system, including all railroads and the main airline. Shall also administer all licensing and registration and shall build and maintain all public transportation routes.

Department of Utilities— will build, maintain, manage, and operate all national utilities.

Treasury Department— will store all funds necessary to operate the executive branch.
   Executive Accounting Office— shall keep track of Executive spending and file reports to the president and National Reserve.

National Reserve

The Reserve shall *independently print, store, release, allot, and gather all money necessary to maintain the entire operations of the nation. Through allotment, it shall ensure that governmental spending is not constrictive toward commercial growth. Also, it shall engineer a stable economic atmosphere through fair monetary distribution. (*However, the Reserve shall also be answerable to the Supreme Court of Governmental Affairs should the House of Provincial Senators petition the Court regarding questionable and/or austere actions planned by the Reserve.)

Director— shall appoint and command all heads of all subordinate offices. Shall determine when the nation's economic atmosphere warrants the printing of additional currency. Shall set the surcharge rate for acquisition of revenue by examining the annual projected budget and accounting reports from all head governmental offices and by examining all other pertinent information. Shall practice monetary-stabilization measures when necessary by releasing or withholding currency or by raising or lowering surcharge or interest rates. Shall determine the amount of currency put onto the international market as well as the safe limit of government bonds to be sold.

Director's Staff— self-explanatory.

(National Monetary Offices)

Office of Monetary Management— shall help the director establish the overall monetary policy by aiding in decisions regarding monetary allotments, surcharge and interest rates, currency released and withheld, the amount of bonds sold, corrective economic actions, and regarding international monetary affairs.

Banking Management and Investment Office— shall determine the main focal points of investment for the nation's banks so that the citizenry's savings will always bear the greatest chance of garnering wholesome interest rates. Shall also continuously seek to improve the banks' operating procedures and will aid in staffing the banking system with the best personnel.

NDC Budgeting Office— shall examine the projected budget reports, accounting reports, and other documents from the National Directive Conglomerate in order to establish a reasonably adequate budget which the NDC will be compelled to follow. The budget will also be set for the Reserve, with the Reserve's budgeting report being filed with the Supreme Court of Governmental Affairs.

OCC Budgeting Office— self-explanatory.

Monetary and Postal Printing Office— shall print all of the nation's currency at the behest of the director. Shall also print all needed postage stamps and postal materials.

National Vault— shall store the nation's unreleased currency as well as its official precious metals and gems.

TBA Office— self-explanatory. Shall file accounting report with the Supreme Court of Governmental Affairs.

(National Reserve's Bureau of Distribution)

National Banking System— shall handle all of the nation's routine banking duties.

Division of Sustenance Distribution— will operate facilities that store sustenance in its raw form and that market it to the individual citizens, to commercial business, and to the government. Will collect, for the National Reserve, all monies that are derived from sales of said sustenance.

Division of Resource Distribution— will operate facilities that store raw resources and that market them to the individual citizens, to commercial business, and to the government. Will collect, for the National Reserve, all monies that are derived from sales of said resources. The resources distributed shall also include fuels (processed by the CCIO).

Division of Utilities Collection— shall collect money from utility bills.

Division of Rent Collection— shall collect all rent paid by tenants of government-built housing or housing governmentally controlled as well as collect all rent paid by the citizenry for use of anything else governmentally controlled.

Division of Transportation Collection— shall collect all money paid by the citizenry for public transportation (including such things as parking fees). Shall also store licensing and registration fees collected by the Department of Transportation.

Division of Penalties Collection— shall receive all money collected by officials concerning fines and penalties.

National Postal Service— shall handle all normal postal services.

OFFICIAL CITIZENS' CONGLOMERATE

The Official Citizen's Conglomerate (OCC) will function as the facilitator which allows the citizenry to explore the more intriguing aspects of life. Its offices will be more accessible to the general public and thereby will receive from it more direct interactional influence. Its functions will be essential, complimentary, and progressive and will include serving as the main link between the people and legislation, serving as the people's watchdog over government and as their voice <u>to</u> government, interpreting the law and Constitution, protecting the nation domestically, progressively distributing the economic and natural resources, stimulating creativity, mass manufacturing much of the nation's needed items, ameliorating the lives of the citizenry, and giving direction and purpose to human endeavor.

Council of the People

(Congregational Branch)

House of Provincial Councilors:

Provincial Councillors— elected by their individual provinces. Shall operate the forum where citizens may voice their concerns to government. The councillors shall hear a variety of concerned citizens, determine the basic national sentiment, and then use this input to determine the best issues to put before the legislature. The House will have the power to initiate progressive national programs that do not interfere with essential official action. The councillors shall have access to information from the prime councillor and may pass their own actions or veto those of the prime councillor with a 60% vote. The chief councillor (elected by the House) shall lead all activity, keep order at sessions, shall render occasional speeches to the House of Provincial Senators, head up the House's required reports, and shall appoint the Printing Office and TBA Office heads.

Council's Printing Office— shall produce all OCC printed literature.

TBA Office— self-explanatory.

(Interactive Branch)

Prime Councillor— shall take steps to improve the contentment of the nation, to ameliorate the difficulties of daily living, to increase and improve pathways for individual and national advancement, and shall establish national programs accordingly. Shall appoint and supervise the heads of all subordinate offices and shall command the operations of the nation's domestic military forces.

Prime Councillor's Staff— self-explanatory.

Prime Councillor's Offices of Policy:

Office of Human Relations— shall aid the prime councillor in various manners dealing with making the lives of the citizenry more comfortable and fulfilling and shall shape policies and develop programs accordingly. Office employees shall interact with the public to determine the average sentiment. Main goals shall be to ease stress and tension, create a more congenial climate of human interaction, and to allow more outlets for entertaining relief. Some specific plans the Office may pursue: public arbitration for those not seeking court action, free information-networks, helping adults and kids find compatible mates and friends, free counselling, and constructive programs to entertain kids after school.

Office of Human Advancement— shall lay the groundwork for the evolution of societal capabilities. Shall orchestrate specific plans with long-range goals geared toward propelling the citizenry to new heights of achievement by certain dates; shall thereby aid the prime councillor in deciding the directions that the Interactive divisions shall pursue regarding general research and exploration. Some general plans: the designing of more capable automated systems that further free humanity for more cerebral as well as social and leisurely endeavors, the development of cheaper and better water purification and desalination processes, the pursuit of processes to transform all waste into usable products, the orchestration of innovative programs of rehabilitation in prison designed to better reform inmates, the planning of cities with improved ecological and practical qualities, and the engineering of mechanisms that more efficiently harvest the energies produced by natural forces.

Board of Holistic Incorporators— shall study man and nature the world over to determine if policies and systems applied by natural forces and by other human cultures produce results superior to the policies and systems practiced domestically. Shall lay the groundwork for incorporating the better ways into the lives of the citizenry.

Office of Economic Advancement— shall continuously devise new and stimulating economic avenues for the nation to collectively and individually explore in its endeavor to prosper. Shall also engineer the most efficient means to manage money regarding the operation of programs and regarding proposals submitted by all offices and divisions of the prime councillor. Possible plans: 1) devising a very efficient barter system for those with commodities but without excessive monetary funds, 2) determining the feasibility of having an apparatus custom-made for a project as compared to purchasing a somewhat less desirable one already on the market, 3) helping the private and governmental sectors combine their capabilities in order accomplish objectives more economically and efficiently, and 4) spotting trends that could generate good profits for investors.

Office of Legal Incorporation— shall ensure that all aspects of all programs are legally sound when they are incorporated into general society. Shall also aid the prime councillor in legal affairs.

Office of Domestic Defense— shall aid in the shaping of policy regarding military action inside national borders and regarding the best weapons designs to pursue.
TBA Office— self-explanatory.

Prime Councillor's Interactive Divisions:

Division of Patents, Trademarks, and Copyrights— shall issue these three documents of intellectual protection to the citizenry. For a minimal fee, inventors shall submit ideas in common language; if the ideas are worthy of patent protection, the Patent Office personnel shall transform the common language into the necessary legal jargon, whereupon the inventions are protected for a standard period of years at no additional cost to the inventors. Patents, copyrights, and trademarks will be protected by law free of charge (the Division shall staff its own authorities to determine infractions).

Research and Development Agency— shall be staffed with scientists, engineers, physicians, experts, and laboratory technicians in all areas of science and technology who are dedicated to finding discoveries and broadening the knowledge base in their various areas. The agency shall command all related facilities necessary for operations and will also work with public and private concerns desiring to expand the horizons of general knowledge.

Division of Behavioral Sciences— shall staff doctors, psychologists and psychiatrists in all areas concerning human behavior who are dedicated to unlocking the mysteries of the human psyche and to applying such knowledge to the task of creating an environment of positive, instead of negative, societal influences. Shall work with prisoners in order to discover ways of preventing crime and with the mentally ill in order to determine the causes of their afflictions. Shall command all facilities necessary for Division operations and shall also work with public and private concerns involved in general research.

Division of Education Advancement— shall staff professionals knowledgeable in general fields along with educational and communications experts who shall continually seek to develop improved methods of education capable of accelerating learning and keeping up with man's increasing knowledge base. Shall possess the facilities necessary to transfer their methods directly to usable medium. Shall also work with public and private concerns involved in developing effective teaching methods.

Agency for Space Exploration— Shall staff all related experts who shall study the cosmos and exploit the boundaries of outer space. Shall command facilities related to the manufacturing and operation of space apparatus. Shall launch all the nation's public, commercial, and exploratory space-bound orbital objects. Shall also work with public and private concerns who harbor benevolent intentions toward space study and exploration.

Library of Human Advancement— shall store all information concerning human discovery and shall distribute such information to requesters.

Master Documented Program— shall serve as one part of the plan to unify mankind. Shall be cataloged and stored within Library (of Human Advancement) walls. The MDP shall list and detail in encyclopedic volume all of man's endeavors to advance his species, all significant problems needing alleviation, all employment available regarding such, and all aid available as well as all organizations which any individual may join concerning their particular interests.

Division of Program Coordination— shall command all facilities and personnel necessary to operate progressive domestic programs enacted by the prime councillor and/or the House of Provincial Councillors. Shall catalog a list and description of programs so that the public and potential volunteers and participants may be informed.

Division of Child Supervision— shall staff and operate orphanages, adoption agencies, and day care facilities that keep children for working parents. Shall also supervise juvenile delinquents.

Collective Earth Organization— shall serve as the ecumenical leg of the plan for uniting mankind's endeavors, functioning as the international haven for Earth's advocates of collective global undertakings. Shall function, for the Council of the People, as its brain trust and outlet for conceiving and enacting progressive nonpolitical and unofficial programs in needy foreign lands. The nation will allot a tract of land as well as all essential facilities that will allow the initial organizational membership—consisting of diversely talented foreign and domestic representatives of all races—to congregate in reasonable comfort and to conduct private and isolated exercises, experiments and conferences dealing with worldly amelioration and advancement, all in a colony-type setting (a "world embassy"). All members must sign an oath committing themselves to congenial cooperation with all other members and to the obedience of the organizational charter. The organization's director shall be elected by the membership and will oversee all proposals submitted to the prime councillor and the provincial councillors for approval and backing. The organization will also be allowed to accept global donations and will pursue perennial goals dedicated to maximizing human synergism, such as: 1) the development and promotion of a common language consisting of global influences (so that all humans may communicate in a nonpartisan language), 2) the establishment and promotion of a constitution for the equity and advancement of all nations (with the conditions for becoming a beneficiary nation being based upon the adherence to ecological compatibility and the respect for human rights), 3) a set of detailed and documented projects for the advancement and development of specific locales. The organizational headquarters shall be established in the domestic nation with the hope that subordinate branches will be allowed to spread to other global areas.

Prime Councillor's Military Agencies:

National Guard— shall defend the nation and keep the peace within national boundaries. Shall operate the Coast Guard and shall provide manpower for national emergencies and disaster relief.

Domestic Weapons Agency— shall design, develop, and manufacture all domestic military weaponry.

Agency for Disaster Relief— shall manage domestic operations in the wake of disasters and shall organize and supervise all military, official, and civil manpower.

Conglomerate of Commercial and Industrial Operations

The CCIO will function as the heart of the nation's production base, with its main purpose being that of providing small but creative entrepreneurs with an alternative outlet for the production and marketing of their creations. It will help tool up private industry and will also produce much of the nation's needed civil and governmental items.

Director— shall appoint and oversee all heads of all subordinate offices. Shall give final clearance as to the best products to be produced by the Conglomerate. Shall give final clearance on the annual reports for obtaining funds and resources. Shall serve as the national and international representative for the nation's commercial and industrial operations.

Director's Staff— self-explanatory.

Executive Board of Advisors— shall consist of the heads of the various offices and divisions who shall frequently collaborate with the director in order to map out strategies and discuss Conglomerate business.

(Divisions of Industry and Commerce)

Office of Product Selection— shall determine which products produced by private creators are deserving of Conglomerate production or aid and shall administer binding contracts between commercial parties and the Conglomerate. A minimal fee will be charged to said private creators in order to prevent a flood of whimsical submissions. The Office shall also determine the quantity of products to be made in reference to available Conglomerate resources and in reference to information from the Product Marketing Agency.

Division of Research and Development— shall staff technological personnel who shall develop and refine all product ideas submitted by all offices of the Conglomerate. The Division shall draft working plans or formulas so that prototypes or samples may be made and tested to ensure items are worthy of Conglomerate production.

Office of Facilities Allotment— shall assign either private firms or governmental personnel and facilities to the task of producing various commercial products. Whenever possible, commercial concerns charging the most reasonable production costs shall be awarded the projects.

Office of Resource Management— will purchase all of the Conglomerate's raw resources from the National Reserve and shall store them and manage their distribution so that all individual production offices are supplied according their allotted limits. (The Conglomerate will pass the cost of resources on to the consumers when products are marketed to private parties.)

Division of Commercial Production— shall command massive manufacturing and production facilities which allow Conglomerate employees to produce products for private parties when private industry is not available or does not possess the capabilities for production. Shall also command tracts of land which allow additional facilities to be supplied for private use until private industry can be found. Shall produce machinery and apparatus with which it shall tool up private industry until the nation is saturated with commercial-production capabilities in diverse categories. Said machinery and apparatus shall either be rented or bought by the private parties. When manufacturing products for domestic commercial concerns and also when providing machinery, the Division shall operate on a break-even basis, with the wholesale prices being designed to cover Conglomerate expenses for machinery and any owed royalties to creators. This elimination of Conglomerate profits will allow the entrepreneurs to reap as high a profit ratio as possible and may help citizens to become stimulated into creativity because of the increased potential for earnings.

Division of Commercial Sustenance Production— will produce food products for private concerns when private industry is not available.

Office of Quality Control— will oversee the quality and safety of all products under Conglomerate jurisdiction before they are released to the market or to their users.

Product Marketing Agency— shall wholesale Conglomerate products to commercial concerns and keep records of such transactions and/or product performances in order to determine which items to continue. The Agency shall store these finished products until they are marketed or recycled. On big-ticket items, some private dealers will be licensed to sell on consignment and will not have to purchase the merchandise. (The Office of Economic Balance shall ensure a fair distribution of wholesale and consignment dealerships.) The Agency will also maintain records of the complete national market for Conglomerate referral.

Citizens' Advertising Agency— shall utilize the Citizens' Media Network to advertise products produced under Conglomerate jurisdiction and to provide small entrepreneurs with affordable advertising. Shall also aid in the production of affordable commercials and graphic layouts.

Division of Civil and Governmental Production— shall command the facilities and personnel necessary to produce all nonmilitary civil and governmental items (including fuels). Shall handle the bulk of the nation's recycling. Shall process the nation's official precious metals which are to be stored in the National Vault. The Division will also manufacture a line of low-end but adequate basic household appliances for those with low incomes renting government housing.

Office of Civil and Governmental Design— shall design efficient structures, products and components for civil and governmental use.

Office of Industrial Design— shall develop more efficient and less expensive production methods for the Conglomerate. Shall design production layouts for the Conglomerate and for commercial concerns. Shall design machinery capable of performing distinct functions for the Conglomerate and for the tooling up of private industry.

Office of Foreign Design— shall aid entrepreneurs in designing products to be sold in foreign lands in order for the nation to better compete in international trade. The Conglomerate's complete facilities shall be open to all foreigners, with the stipulation being that all items designed and developed free of charge must be produced under Conglomerate control and that all foreign marketing shall be done exclusively through the International Trade Agency. The Conglomerate can also be paid by foreigners to perform any and all functions. (Note: The availability of the Conglomerate for hire to foreigners will serve as another currency-backing commodity, further securing the domestic currency's value as the Conglomerate's capabilities increase and advance. As gold is a currency-backing commodity, so is production capability.)

International Trade Agency— shall handle all the routine burdens of marketing all of the nation's exported and imported finished commercial goods. Shall maintain records of all exported products and shall control and operate outlets on domestic soil which shall be the only places where imported goods can be initially sold inside national boundaries.

TBA Office— self-explanatory.

Official Citizens' Independent Agencies

Office of Economic Balance— basic intent will be that of ensuring a fair and wide distribution of the wealth and of preventing the occurrences of monopolies and oligarchies capable of destabilizing the nation's economy. Shall continuously consult the Census Agency statistics and will scope the national economic atmosphere to spot citizens who are at the lower ends of the monetary scale in an effort to incorporate them into lucrative endeavors capable of bringing them better economic success, especially so that locales of concentrated poverty cannot develop. Shall discourage monopolies and oligarchies in certain commercial markets by temporarily competing directly in the markets or by capitalizing competition against businesses that it feels are excessively powerful. Shall ensure the existence of a fair and pervasive dealership base consisting of private manufacturers who sell finished commercial goods manufactured under government supervision. Shall ensure that government institutions are built on a pervasive basis nationally so that all areas will benefit economically. (Shall use the Court of Governmental Affairs to gain compliance.) Shall oversee a subordinate office (**Foreign Goods Regulatory Office**) which shall keep track of the balance of trade (as conducted by the International Trade Agency) and which shall advise when protective action is to be taken.

National Agency of Investigation— shall investigate all governmental offices and have access to all governmental records in order to ensure that all officials are operating scrupulously, efficiently and competently. Shall use the Court of Governmental Affairs in order to pursue prosecution. Shall also investigate all matters of wide-range national importance.

Commission of Election and Recall— shall serve as the center for the general citizenry to express their approval or disapproval of provincial and national officials. On the national level, each provincial Commission shall monitor the approval ratings of all national officials; when 50% indicate an official as having a severe disapproval rating, the national Commission shall warn the official and grant them a period of time to improve in ratings before conducting an election allowing the people an opportunity to replace the official. The Commission shall administer the funds for all election campaigns and shall conduct elections to find replacements for positions vacated for any reason. The approval ratings for governmental appointees shall also be monitored. Governmental laws, actions, and projects awarded through public land votes will also face the threat of being recalled upon accumulating adequate public disapproval.

Land Allotment Commission— will ensure the citizens and government of fair and balanced land distribution necessary for adequate civillan activities, governmental operations, and ecological preservation.

Resource Allotment Commission— will ensure a climate of fair access to the nation's exploitable raw resources by examining all evidence of the nation's projected needs in order to grant reasonable portions to individual citizens, commercial business, and to government.

Sustenance Allotment Commission— shall ensure a climate of fair access to the nation's governmentally produced/controlled sustenance by examining all evidence of the nation's projected needs in order to grant reasonable portions to individual citizens, commercial business, and to government.

Production Inspection Agency— shall approve or disapprove governmental and commercial products based upon their safeness or danger potential. Shall report the best and worst quality products in order to inform consumers.

Arts, Media, and Entertainment Regulatory Commission— will establish and oversee regulations and policies regarding the arts, publications, film, television and radio programs, the Internet, and broadcasting and station sales and transactions. Shall control the ratings system and shall set censoring policies. Shall commission channels and frequencies.

Citizens' Media Network— shall especially aid the little man in media concerns. Shall offer TV/radio programming and printed literature serving the public interest. Will control and manage Internet access. Will function as an alternative to commercialized media.

National Judiciary System

Supreme Court of Governmental Affairs— shall serve as the ultimate court of appeals for cases tried in the lower Courts of Governmental Affairs. Shall consist of multiple judges elected by the people who shall simultaneously sit on a common bench and vote on decisions upon reviewing evidence. Will decide if proper governmental action has been taken in relation to constitutional law, shall render decision as to whether officials at the national level should be indicted and whether charges should be filed in criminal court thereby, shall settle civil disputes between the government and the citizenry, and shall settle inner-governmental disputes. Shall serve as the only court in the nation that settles disputes concerning the granting of extra funding and resources to governmental branches (shall decide by determining whether the shift in assets would improve or impede the nation's overall stability). Shall also serve as the regulator of actions taken by the National Reserve.

Supreme Court of Civil and Criminal Affairs— All judges shall be elected. Shall function as the ultimate interpreter of the Constitution and its laws and as the ultimate court of appeals regarding criminal cases and regarding civil cases in which the government is not the significant plaintiff or defendant.

Judicial Commissioners— shall appoint all judges below the supreme courts. Shall also monitor judges' performances and decisions. Commissioners are elected.

Commissioners of Trial Jurors— shall commission those citizens most qualified to serve as trial jurors. Citizens shall be tested for psychological fitness and their individual verdicts shall be monitored over a period of time in order to determine if a pattern of biasness exists that warrants termination of their commissions. Juristic service will be a professional occupation on a part- or full-time basis; it will be offered as a two-year college major (with course requirements such as basic law, psychology, and detective basics) and jurors will be selected by lottery for trials. This service will also serve as a method for attorneys to repay the government for their education. In cases of juror shortages, the general citizenry will be eligible to be drafted in order to accommodate the difference, but the commission process should relieve the majority of the public from this unpopular burden. (Commissioners are elected.)

Commissioners of Panel Members— shall commission criminal court panel members, who shall be used in lieu of individual attorneys to question subjects in trials and also used optionally in lieu of juries to render verdicts.

All other needed, lower courts covering all other matters shall be included in the judicial branch. The judges will be appointed.

Chapter 3

PROPOSED CATEGORICAL BREAKDOWN

(Note: These are proposals only. Any subsequent,
superior, ideas will be later incorporated.)

Abortion

Legal in the first trimester. Provided free of charge by government in cases of youth, rape, incest, extreme fetal physical complications, danger to mother, or for the accommodation of population-control policy. For abortions not of these cases, funding could come from the individuals involved or from a governmental choice-fund which allows voluntary contributions so that the service is available on a socialistic basis for citizens of lower income.

(Note: In order to decrease the desire for abortion, along with better birth-control methods, the nation shall seek to develop increasingly sophisticated life-support systems—"substitute wombs"—capable of sustaining the fetus outside of the mother at earlier and earlier stages of life. This alternative will be offered to mothers so that they may end their pregnancies early without terminating the fetus, allowing the baby to develop and be adopted.)

Alcohol and Tobacco

I personally consider these substances as drags upon the human race, with tobacco especially being a nasty, filthy habit. But the personal sentiment of some should not dictate the individual rights of others. And, as long as both the legal rights of the partakers and the abstainers are respected, then the partakers should be allowed to practice whatever vices they wish.

Because these are nonessential and potentially detrimental elements, the amount of land and resources devoted to their production shall be voted on by the public. The private sector will engineer its own mixtures regarding ingredients, but the government will produce the finished products as well as all crops and paraphernalia associated with the production and packaging of both indulgences—paid for by the investors of the said private sector.

A special surcharge—"national health liability insurance"—will be charged to the private investors, which they will pass on to consumers. The liability system will cover substance-related medical care (regardless of whether it is governmentally or commercially provided), civil suits, fines, as well as rehab for people wanting to break their addictions—with separate stipulations for smoking and drinking, of course. If detrimental societal effects increase, the surcharge will be increased as well.

Distribution centers will be established where the government can track all circulation and sales. These centers will wholesale the items in bulk to licensed businesses (bars, liquor stores, nightclubs, restaurants, etc.) Individual dealers must have a registered place of business and will be fined for selling outside of its boundaries or for selling to the under aged. Public smoking restrictions will be strictly enforced. Media advertising will be stringently monitored in order to ensure that no deceptions are carried on regarding health consequences and that the substances are not portrayed as glamorous or "socially necessary."

Arts and Entertainment

The government will be allowed one national TV network, one national newspaper, and one FM radio network accessible to all areas of the nation— Citizens' Media Network (CMN). The CMN will serve to keep the populace informed of current events and will be a source of information for important topics as well as a provider of entertainment; interviews will be conducted with important political figures, and it shall serve to educate everyone at all age levels about the world and man. Small business will receive national exposure for low cost, and all businesses that significantly aid the government in serving the people will be given free advertising. Examples: Businesses that are willing to hire ex-offenders or who donate large sums to charities will receive governmental advertising-incentives.

On TV, small production companies will be given air time by the CMN so that their new shows can run nationwide. Their shows will each run for a limited number of weeks, most effectively during the rerun stage of commercial television. The commercial sector will judge and then bid on any desired shows.

On radio, small recording companies and little-known artists will be given air time so that their talent can be exposed. Also, little-known political activists—or anyone in general having something interesting to contribute— will be featured.

In the newspaper, lesser known columnists and cartoonists will be given space, and a missing-persons and most-wanted section will run continuously.

Internet access: available for free to all (just as one pays nothing when one turns on the radio to hear free music). The government will provide the access while using the most advanced methods available. Internet access will be funded by advertisers and site owners who pay the government to post Web sites. Free access will save money and stimulate economic growth.

In order to assure low advertising rates, the government will subsidize the CMN if necessary, but the initial goal will be for it to operate on a break-even basis.

The commercial sector will control the rest of the market and will have free reign in handling all major entertainment and celebrities. For the launching of broadcast satellites, the commercial sector must patronize the government (Agency for Space Exploration); by law, it shall possess the only such facilities. Both the governmental and commercial sectors must obey the rules and regulations of the Arts, Media, and Entertainment Regulatory Commission. (Note: This may be a much more awesome and involving responsibility than one may immediately realize, because we cannot be sure as to the extent to which the hypnotic images blaring from our screens or the evocative lyrics and sounds resonating from radio waves and electronic recording devices affect the minds of all exposed. Such regulation requires the application of psychological experimentation and sociological studies as well as decision based merely on empirical data.)

Banking

Totally governmentally controlled in order to eliminate the threat of private greed, scandals, and nonregulated and incompetent decision regarding the bulk of the nation's money. This will also serve to limit personnel salaries so that more bank money will be available for the people to exploit. The government (Banking Management and Investment Office) will have access to the best information and the best business minds in order to guide the banking system into making the soundest investments.

Unlike the capitalist one, the main purpose of the semisocialistic banking system is to spread loaned money efficaciously throughout the populace and to serve as the watchdog over it assuring its return. Since bank personnel will be salaried governmental employees, the banks' interest rate will be strategically set to grant reasonable returns to depositors and to operate all banks on a break-even basis so that borrowing will be encouraged and so that the public will be awarded adequate gains on their accounts. Those banking executives most successful at lending the most money while breaking even at their individual banks will be promoted within the system. The banks will be aggressive at aiding the public through business networking.

Free electronic monetary transfers will be available for all citizens holding checking or savings   accounts. Also, an online financial transaction system will allow account holders to swap money back and forth at no cost—to help accommodate rapid commerce and expand economic activity.

Regarding financial matters, the commercial sector may own loan and investment companies and the like, but they may not offer regular banking services.

Business

The commercial sector may compete with the government in every area of business that is not used to gather the nation's revenue. It will totally control all domestic retailing of domestic goods and will have access to exploiting all forms of the service industry that the government does not touch. The commercial sector will be given the first chance to manufacture new commercial products, but the government (CCIO) shall manufacture all products too large or complex for the granted private land space and shall also manufacture all items used by government. The private sector will completely control the stock market as well as all private bonds. To protect the public against phony businesses, individuals operating private businesses under a business name must register with an office of the government—probably an office in the National Reserve.

Since, for a healthy economy, the quantity of released currency in circulation is proportional to the amount of goods and services available, only established businesses who aid the National Reserve in determining said amount will be eligible for special governmental-incentives such as networking services, preferred contracts and loans, cheap advertising, etc. Plus, the allotment agencies and the Reserve will offer cheaper, bulk prices for parties who comply. These incentives will compel the private sector to fill out forms indicating the type of business, the materials used, and the quantities and prices of the various items sold or services rendered. Since this process is so simple and does not call for the businesses to pay additional taxes, compliance should be given congenially. (To participate, the business owners must be "pure entrepreneurs"—not employed in any way by any other entity, governmental or private. (This eliminates any chance of them being coerced to get products for their employers at cheaper prices.)

Capital Punishment

Not applied—unless the homicidal criminal possess such an ability to escape that all existing methods available to confine him or her are rendered completely ineffective. Murderers sentenced to life with no hope of parole may request self-applied life termination—which could comprise their being led into a private chamber, whereupon they may voluntarily consume a lethal substance designed to cause death as quickly and painlessly as possible.

Credit Industry

The credit industry will be required to register all activities and customers with a credit-check agency of the government. Before being issued any card, consumers will have to fill out a form declaring their income level, whereupon the agency will impose a credit limit—for all cards collectively that are held by a single consumer (to prevent consumers from using multiple cards to get further into debt). Citizens desiring a higher limit will be required to bring proof of higher income (pay records, bank accounts, etc.) Consumers who falsely magnify their incomes in order to expand their credit limit and, as a result, cannot repay their issued credit will be subject to civil action from businesses, criminal fraud charges, or to other actions.

Day Care

Provided free of charge governmentally (Division of Child Supervision). The center will provide supervision, toys, and entertainment; the parents must provide food, milk, diaper paraphernalia, and other needs they prefer their children to have or a fee will be charged. An inspector will visit the center to watch for signs of incompetence, abuse, and violations. The commercial sector may participate in day care but will also be liable to governmental inspection.

Deaths: Laying to Rest

Because land space is precious—and finite—all deceased citizens laid to rest within national boundaries shall be cremated. This will be the law—no matter one's religion or beliefs. Those objecting will have to explore the option of having their deceased loved ones taken elsewhere. Regarding cremation, a possible idea would be for the government to build mortuary structures comprised of small drawers that visitors may open, with said drawers bearing the vase of ashes along with pictures, biographic literature, and personal items of the departed; a small one-time fee would be charged for this. The funeral process will be a non-governmental one; the cremation process can be either privately or governmentally performed.

Defense

The executive branch (NDC) will bear the responsibility of protecting the nation from the outside. The inside will be the responsibility of the interactive branch (OCC)—a branch designed to be in touch with and more accessible to the citizenry. All militaristic weapons are to be manufactured solely by governmental personnel. Military recruitment will operate on a volunteer basis, with economic, educational, and special civil privileges serving as incentives to join.

Morally, militaristic strength will never be used for cultural exploitation or unwanted intervention. No assault will be launched on foreign lands on behalf of the nation unless an obvious and imposing peril exists that is absolutely untenable without armed conflict. Mercy missions shall not be joined unless there is global support and participation. Economically, the nation's infrastructure will not suffer excessive military monetary diversion unless the nation is being directly attacked in holocaust proportions. Technologically, new weaponry and procedures will continuously be developed that will allow conflicts to end with minimum bloodshed and that will incapacitate humans while remaining innocuous to the environment.

Disability

For security regarding no-fault injuries which occur outside of work, citizens may take out private or extra governmental insurance to tide them over until recuperation. Uninsured citizens who are injured may receive no-interest governmental loans that they must repay after recovery of health. The permanently or significantly disabled will receive disability payments from the Department of Livelihood.

Displaced Workers

As the nation's human labor is replaced by automation, human potential will be directed into the more complex and advanced endeavors—particularly those of research and development in all fields. Since machines do not need pay, that cash flow shall be re-channeled towards an ever-increasing pool of retrained and expanding minds laboring to find more effective methods of environmental preservation, stronger/lighter/tougher/cheaper materials, better medical treatments, smarter electronic circuits, more efficient fuels, more about the mysteries of the universe, more about the psyche of man, more capable automation....to replace still more human labor—endeavors leading to evolutionary capabilities. Research and development will be the nation's pot of gold—also allowing the nation to grant more and more workers (especially governmental) the amenity of less hours with the same pay.

Government— Will offer select workers on-the-job training or will grant retraining in governmental institutions of learning. The younger employees will be the first selected for retraining while the older sect will be the last manning a job until its obsolescence. Some of the displaced who are of an age unfeasible for retraining but still with significant time before retirement will be offered consignment dealerships to sell governmentally produced goods until reaching retirement and receiving their subsistence checks. Upon retirement, their consignment dealership shall be terminated and they will be eligible for only wholesale dealerships, requiring those choosing to remain in business to expend their own capital for wholesale purchases. The government will also maintain a jobs bank with the private sector, with said jobs bank being for the displaced to consult. Plus, the government will operate a national network that will pervasively circulate job-seekers' resumes for all prospective employees to see.

Private Sector— Individual private concerns shall receive preferential governmental incentives in an amount proportional to the generosity of their employee-retraining programs and to the amount of aid they give their older displaced employees in finding other work or in starting businesses.

Drugs (Narcotics or Recreational)

Treated as a social-health matter. Legal for all adults except pregnant mothers—but only if produced domestically; no "imports" allowed. Marketing must be done discreetly and completely out of public view. The justice system shall be involved only when criminal acts are committed regarding recreational narcotics or committed while the subjects are under drug influence. Pushers selling fatal drugs resulting in death will be prosecuted for homicide. Criminal acts will result in incarceration, lesser penalties, or court-ordered treatment. Since addicted mothers threaten the lives of their unborn, these mothers-to-be will be confined in amiable facilities and treated until the birth of their children, during which time they'll be eligible for a no-interest governmental loan to help tide over their normal living expenses. Identifiable fathers liable for child care will be required to contribute financially to the process. Any father not reporting his pregnant wife or sexual partner for drug usage will endanger his parental rights, will still be held paternally liable, and may even be prosecuted. All governmental/private businesses and organizations will have the right to test employees on a periodic basis or to require the testing of applicants and may terminate or refuse employment to anyone at any time who tests positive. All political officials will be required to remain drug-free and will undergo constant testing. All owners of private places for rent will have the right to refuse tenants known to use drugs. (The government may register chronic users for public protection and reference.) And, of course, drug usage will be a liability in all child-custody cases.

Through research and development, voluntary treatment could include pills which produce lethargic effects (counter-agents) when mixed with narcotics. Voluntary and involuntary treatment could include the development of surgical implants that emit these counter-agents upon activation by narcotics introduced into the bloodstream.

Should drug usage become problematic, the nation's revenue shall be redirected to counter it, with the funds going toward treatment, rehabilitation, and studies to determine why some people would rather live in an inebriated world than a sober one. Problematic chronic users who commit no significant crimes will be confined to large treatments areas, where they will reside in dormitories and be employed until it's believed they can successfully return to society.

The semisocialistic ideology is to acknowledge that some individuals are attracted to drugs, accept it, and to incorporate it into the system in such a way that the overall status of the citizenry is protected from the <u>real</u> threat drugs pose—crime or injury against <u>others</u>. The individual user shouldn't be punished unless he or she threatens the safety and lives of others.

Education

Provided free of charge by the government for all citizens who follow the normal chronological cycle. The behavior-disordered will be provided with the necessary attention at separate facilities. The mentally handicapped will be trained in simplistic skills and trades in which they will work throughout their lives, with this training to be conducted at separate facilities.

From grade school on through the years of higher education, standardized tests will indicate academic achievement and determine when students deserve promotion to advanced subject material and grade levels. Numbered grades will be used to indicate whether students have mastered an acceptable or unacceptable level of the material. If unacceptable, then only that unlearned material will be re-studied until an acceptable level is reached (to take the pressure off the student by eliminating the fear of failing and having to repeat entire courses). When all courses pertaining to a grade level have been successfully completed, the next grade will be entered into immediately. (As students complete individual courses in which they are more gifted, more time will be available for them to study their more challenging ones.)

For the younger children, hyperactivity shall be relieved by eliminating "chair time" more and more—allowing them to have more mobile and physical interaction with their didactic environment. Also, massive effort will be exerted in order to find dynamic and stimulating ways to teach those who learn better through different processes, and teachers will be assigned who specialize in those particular methods. Teachers producing the best results will garner special incentives and privileges. Different schools or sections of same schools will provide the various teaching methods and equipment. For the more disciplined and capable students, a self-pace program will be offered to all who are of enough discipline to make sufficient independent progress, with educational paraphernalia and standardized tests serving as the teacher and as the indicator of achievement.

The first six grade-levels shall consist mainly of reading, writing and math, with reading governing the bulk of the attention. Methods shall be practiced geared toward elevating the students up to a level of rapid reading ability (speed-reading). During this time, their vocabulary shall also be expanded.

Grades seven through nine will introduce a curriculum of advanced math, history, social studies, geography, environmental appreciation, physical education, basic science, nutrition and cooking, and also optional courses such as foreign languages. Emphasis will continue to be placed upon speed-reading and vocabulary (with the intent being, the faster reading occurs, the faster learning occurs, the faster contributions to society occur). Self-pace will be virtually in full effect at these grade levels, and the students will switch from grade to grade as they individually progress.

As students near the end of the ninth-grade level, they'll be given an initial intelligence test and required to rank—in order of preference—a broad list of general fields of study in which they are interested. The junior high schools will provide a condensed library covering all offered fields so that the students may have the adequate information to learn more about them before making selections. Those displaying a higher I.Q. and aptitude will be awarded the more challenging fields, with the high school class size being designed to fill projected national need.

During high school, self-pace education and speed-reading training will continue along with the mandatory and optional courses; study of the awarded field will begin. The high school will be provided with the necessary facilities to teach the complete list of fields that were offered, and the students will have the opportunity to acquire familiarity with their chosen career paths before entering college or tech. school. (This will also give them firsthand experience to decide if they like their choice of fields.) The high school library will contain numerous copies of all material taught in all courses offered. All requesting students will be allowed library time to learn more concerning their first choice or to decide upon another field and begin its study on their own (in addition to studying their awarded field) so that they will not lose time compared to those who have been awarded and are already enrolled in that particular course. As individual students complete their high school education, they'll be given final testing to indicate their knowledge level in their studied field and to determine aptitude. Here, those wishing to switch to a different field (for college or tech. school) and who have adequately studied will have a chance to overtake those who are already studying that particular field by posting superior scores regarding testing pertaining to it. Besides testing, the students will also rank a list of majors within their field of study that they wish to pursue collegiately or technically. The government will examine the test results and award the majors to those best qualified according to a class size strategically determined to be of the volume necessary to accommodate the nation's needed work force. The government will provide complete funding for all required courses in majors.

Upon high school graduation, the students will be granted up to a four-year collegiate and up to a two-year tech. school education free of charge, but only to study their awarded majors; students must provide their own funding for all electives. (No electives will be required.) The entering-class volume will be adjusted as needed by the government, but those already enrolled in their majors will be allowed to continue until graduation. Continuing in action will be self-pace and speed-reading training. Those college students who continuously fail to make adequate progress and who are unresponsive to all practiced forms of instructional aid will be demoted to less challenging chosen college majors on down to their chosen tech. school majors until a compatible major is found. Those in tech. school will be demoted as well. The government college and tech. school will provide each student with all necessary course materials and will provide those from distant locales with free room and board if needed. The government will offer master's and doctorate degree programs to a select few of the highest achieving students in all significant fields, whereupon, after graduation, they will be obligated to serve the nation for minimal salary for an established period of time in government hospitals, in public legal representation, in the military, or in other governmental institutions relevant to their careers. High school graduates who join the military will also be collegiately or technically educated; those with only technical educations will have the option of attending government college as older adults in later years.

The private sector may compete with the government at every level of education but must teach all required courses, harbor all required facilities, and must impose all standardized tests that indicate achievement and that aid the government in projecting the class volumes in college and tech. school. All who choose not to pursue their awarded majors and who seek formal graduate degrees or formal retraining—who weren't selected by the government, or who are older adults seeking formal higher education (who are not military veterans)—will fund their educations from sources outside those of government. Also, those students in governmental colleges selected for graduate studies will have the option of eliminating their obligation to public service by paying their own fees or by spending those extra years in private education.

For those wishing to retrain or obtain higher education without formal supervision, the government will institute a self-education system incorporating computer software and instructional literature that will allow such citizens to accumulate knowledge in as clear and concise a manner as possible. The instructional materials will be available for free on the Internet, on loan through national libraries, or for a price through governmental distribution centers. Students will receive study credits and degrees by taking standardized tests given at various times and locations by government officials.

Legally, it will be mandatory that all citizens (who are not mentally or physically handicapped or who haven't received special dispensation) pursue their education from grade school on through the collegiate or technical level in a normal and uninterrupted chronological cycle regardless of whether the facility is governmental or private. Land bonds and marriage certificates will not be granted until graduation occurs. Young students who chronically misbehave in governmental or private facilities will be subject to detention in juvenile facilities, not to be released until undergoing psychoanalysis, a rigid disciplinary program, and until proven to be potentially productive—or at least safe—for society. Some other possible stipulations are school uniforms (to prevent fad & fashion distractions) and separate facilities for the sexes (to eliminate a sexual distraction from learning and to reduce encounters leading to teen sex).

Elections

Candidates will get onto the ballot by paying an entry fee proportionate to their annual income and the level of office. The Citizens' Media Network will grant equal exposure to all candidates and will list their qualifications, personal history and political platform. The private media must grant equal exposure to all candidates or face possible suits; however, private media may freely report significant news concerning candidates that isn't of a promotional nature.

Provincial elections will be decided simply by popular vote. Candidates running for national offices must first capture their provincial nominations regarding those particular offices. In the general national election, voters will be required to rank a designated minimum quantity of candidates in order of preference. The candidates with the highest national ranking win. (Requiring voters to rank multiple candidates—as compared to allowing them to simply vote for a singular one—will give those candidates from less populous provinces a more fair shot.)

Extra Governmental Funding and Allotments

Any governmental office requesting funding, land, resources, or sustenance in excess of that granted by the Reserve or the allotment commissions must submit a petition to the Supreme Court of Governmental Affairs. The petition will be publicized. If no objections arise from any other offices, those extras will be allotted if possible, with said extras coming from stored supplies, from other governmental offices, or from surcharge increases in specific commodities or services. If objections arise, the Court will weigh all evidence of the substantiality of need, with the burden of proof falling upon the party who submitted the petition requesting the extras.

Facility Expansion

Each citizen will be given a limit of two granted property lots (GPLs) and may claim them upon reaching adulthood and completing educational requirements, whereupon they will be granted private land bonds. All such citizens will be designated as "land representatives" since they'll represent a portion of all land that is legally manipulatable by the citizenry. In order to ensure the availability of land for land-trading and for business expansion, no private structure (on private land not awarded by vote) will exceed one GPL.

Homes— Each GPL will be of a generous size for the average home. Homes may be constructed from any materials that are officially safe and in any legal manner desired by owners.

Business— Entrepreneurs who have maximized their facilities on both their GPLs may approach other land representatives and pay them for the use of their land, but those representatives may not be a member of the entrepreneur's parental or maternal family or a first-generation cousin, uncle, aunt, niece, nephew, in-law, or an employee (to avoid the use of procreation for personal or family greed, to eliminate one avenue for coercion of subordinates, and to spread money more evenly throughout the general populace). If found in violation, then the renting entrepreneur, not the land representative, will face fines and/or confiscation of business paraphernalia. The government (Department of Land Management) will assist in finding legitimate representatives and in checking family background. Contracts between entrepreneurs and representatives will be valid only for a limited number of years before renegotiations so that representatives will be free to change renters or go into business for themselves. Because businesses tend to be less permanent than homes, all business structures will be built in a manner that allows easy assembly (i.e., quick-assembly materials) or disassembly. Representatives may designed them to accommodate stacking (extra stories added), wherein they may choose to rent different levels to different tenants.

Excess Land— Of the excess commercially-exploitable land, the public will be allowed to vote on its usage. Entrepreneurs will submit proposals to the Department of Land Management along with the payment of a candidacy fee (to discourage a flood of whimsical proposals). Their submissions shall encompass such proposals as private learning institutions, sporting stadiums, hospitals, concert halls, amusement parks, and businesses and industries of all allowable kinds. The proposals will list the advantages they bear—such as jobs and economic stimulation—and will be posted online and printed in abridged form in publications made available to the public. The total amount of land up for vote will be indicated by "units," with one unit equaling one GPL; each proposal shall list the number of units its span will cover. When voting (with the voting process being handled by the Commission of Election and Recall), the citizens will rank their choices in order of preference. The winners will be those proposals with the highest rankings whose combined units fall within the limit of the total amount of available units.

Example: One thousand units are up for vote. Candidates are 1) an amusement park—300 units, 2) a private college—400 units, 3) a processing/ canning facility—300 units, 4) a large adult entertainment complex—200 units, 5) a private research and development facility—100 units, and 6) an exercise and athletic complex—100 units. After the vote, the final rankings are: 3—1st, 2—2nd, 4—3rd, 1—5th, and 6—6th. Since proposals 3, 2, and 4 add up to 900 units, only 100 are still available. The next available one which will accommodate this is #5. Therefore, the winners are 3, 2, 4, and 5. The winning entrepreneurs will be exempt from any fees on land usage. At any point in the future, those citizens dissatisfied with the performance of any of the winners may file a form with the Commission of Election and Recall, wherein, if enough are accumulated, another vote will be held in accordance with the unit size of the targeted facility.

Fiscal Management

Currency will be printed according to gross national product (GNP). Its primary release will go toward funding the essential goods and services provided by the semisocialist system. Its second priority will be to the free market. The third priority will be its release to the government-sponsored amenities programs (under the Official Citizens' Conglomerate) designed to grant a higher quality of life to the citizenry. The government will utilize technological development—sponsored largely by its amenities programs—to continuously lower the citizenry's cost of living, thereby making more currency available to the free market. As the free market allows citizens to purchase more government-controlled resources and services, more money will again be available to the amenities programs. And so the cycle starts again to further lower living costs.

In order to hold inflation forever in check, the wages of governmental workers will remain at a constant level relative to their particular positions. Raises for them will be granted only then they earn promotions or are granted senior status. The amount of expendable capital the governmental workers possess in relation to the private sector will serve as the main governor for the release and withholding of currency to and from the economy. If commercial salaries are significantly higher than governmental ones, then the adequate amount of currency would be withheld <u>from</u> the commercial economy. If they're significantly lower, then the projected needed additional amount would be released <u>to</u> it. (Let us also remember the government's responsibility to monitor the economic landscape regarding the nation's needed future workforce so that it can fulfill that need via collegiate and technical education.)

As government work becomes increasingly technical and automation eliminates and alters jobs, those remaining higher-skilled positions will command the applicable higher wages needed to attract the required workers, thereby ensuring a steady, available government workforce.

Also regarding fiscal management, the governmental amenities programs will constantly host projects, along with research-and-development ventures, where money could be directed and used—which would thereby allow said projects and ventures to constitute a portion of the GNP. This allows another option for inflation control: Instead simply of withholding currency from the economy to control commercial-wage inflation, the government could simply redirect more of it <u>away</u> from the commercial sector and <u>toward</u> the governmental sector.

Hopefully, this scheme, along with the incorporation of a system of fair and equitable wealth-distribution, will prevent all domestic economic difficulties and, in the process, virtually eliminate the need for significant corrective fiscal action.

Gambling

If there is to be gambling—whether casino or lottery—it will be conducted by the government, with the proceeds going to the nation's pool of revenue (thereby reducing the National Reserve's revenue surcharge). Gamblers will acquire electronic debit cards from the government and debit them at amounts not exceeding a limit, based upon their monthly income, designed to prevent personal over-expenditure. The card will bear the gambler's photograph, and he/she will be the only ones allowed to use it. At all gambling and lottery facilities, the clerks will verify the photographs and insert the cards into electronic checking and debiting devices The users will type in the PIN number, and the value of the cards will decrease according to the quantity of chips or lottery tickets purchased.

Guns

All handguns will be banned from the general public and issued exclusively to police, military personnel, and to other official figures. Only the government (Division of Civil and Governmental Production) will manufacture handguns. The general public will be banned from commanding any assault or heavy firearm of any kind. All private firearms will equal or exceed thirty-six inches in length, will fire no more than six rounds, and will be of a reasonable caliber for protection, with reasonable allowances for hunting. The commercial sector will manufacture all such weaponry for the general populace, with the Department of Law Enforcement serving as the watchdog.

Health

All essential health and medical care in every category will be available through socialized care. Every general citizen will be granted one free checkup every two years. All other visitations initiated by the citizens in a shorter period of time will result in a billing unless a significant disorder is found (in order to discourage whimsical visits). All prescription drugs, medicines, and paraphernalia will be gratis and obtainable directly through the hospital or governmental distribution centers. Promotions and raises will be awarded based upon those medical personnel who render the healthiest patients while applying the most efficient use of medical resources. (Note: This form of socialized practice should virtually eliminate the dangerous cutting of corners and the corrupt padding of bills as compelled by the profit motive in capitalism.)

The government will handle mental cases that are only of enough significance to cause detrimental side effects. The government will handle cosmetic cases only in extreme cases of deformity or in occurrences caused by accident. All essential research by hospitals and by the Research and Development Agency will be adequately supported by the government.

The commercial sector may offer every health services and pursue every field of research as the government but must comply with all governmental regulations. It will control all over-the-counter drugs and medicines; it will also handle all routine cosmetic cases and milder mental cases. Should commercial research ever yield a drug or discovery that is critically needed by the nation, the government may appropriate its usage as it sees fit but must adequately compensate the commercial party. For population-control purposes, the government and the commercial sectors must report all child births to the National Census Agency.

Housing

The bulk of all housing will be commercially or individually provided. The government (Department of Livelihood) will build and provide housing on a break-even basis for all lower-income citizens who cannot afford to buy or build according to market price, wherein some housing will be pre-built and set aside for that purpose. To help preserve forests, the governmental housing will be built from artificial, quick-assembly materials that are durable, and they could also be designed to resemble traditional or standard building materials. And, as much as possible, all such materials will be fireproof. All who are governmentally housed will pay an affordable rent on a rent-to-own basis. The property containing the government home will be considered one GPL, but the renter-owner will have full rights to his/her other allotted lot.

For large governmental industrial/civil facilities, reserved housing for employees could be provided near said facilities in order to decrease the need for the employees to travel long distances to said facilities. This would reduce energy usage, save time, and would also help relieve general traffic congestion. Residents would purchase the housing, counting as one GPL. Residents retired from or no longer employed by the facilities would be required to move if the housing is needed by other employees, but the retired residents would be reimbursed.

If there is competition between parties in any national community to own the same home, the home will be granted to the party possessing the occupational skills most needed by that particular community.

Immigration

Allowed so long as the nation's population quantity is under the limit. The Bureau of Immigration and Naturalization will monitor immigrant numbers to ensure that the quantity obeys a strict limit that prevents an unmanageable rise in the nation's total population.

Insurance

Health— There is no need for it unless private care is preferred by the citizen, wherein commercial insurance must be sought. The government will insure its doctors free of charge and the medical staff will be disciplined, dismissed or decertified if found sufficiently incompetent. Civil review boards may be employed to decide if patients have legitimate cases. Private doctors must seek private insurance regarding liability.

Housing— All government-supplied housing rented to the citizenry, as well as all included appliances, will be governmentally insured via replacement. Since the government will only ensure the availability of basic housing, all citizens who own the more luxurious commercially built residences will seek the private insurance sector for full coverage.

Vehicles— Totally commercially controlled, but must be set on a no-fault basis concerning accidents. Accident-prone drivers will be required to pay to attend traffic school or may choose to compensate the injured party. Chronically bad drivers may have their licenses revoked. Rates will not increase for those who simply violate traffic laws. Instead, the violators will merely be fined or penalized. A possible idea to motivate good driving: Reward good drivers with insurance rebate checks accumulated from fines applied to penalized drivers.

Personal Items— All items purchase on the free market will be commercially insured.

Businesses— Totally commercially controlled.

Life— Totally commercially controlled.

(Note: If it is ever found by the Office of Economic Balance that any area of commercial insurance is too highly priced, then the Office will induce lower prices by either stepping in and selling the necessary types of insurance directly to the public or by widening the field of competition by funding the establishment of additional commercial firms.)

International Trade and Aid

Whenever possible, the nation will engineer the use of its resources in a manner that will allow it to operate with self-sufficiency in the bulk of its endeavors. No other nation should be allowed to infiltrate the domestic economy to the point that no form of "protectionism" could be enacted against those who practice unfair trade. The Foreign Goods Regulatory Office will serve as the protecting concern. Citizens wishing to trade internationally and foreigners desiring to trade with the nation may do so only through the International Trade Agency. Businesspeople wishing to establish enterprises in foreign nations must use foreign facilities and will not be allowed to export resources, sustenance, or facilities unless given special permission by the government. As said, the Department of Resource Management will internationally trade the nation's more plentiful resources for the less abundant ones. The Department of Sustenance will also internationally swap goods. The nation's official precious metals and gems (National Vault) will serve as added currency backers and as securities that can be released to the international market should the nation suffer disasters, emergencies, or economic difficulties.

The Reserve and allotment commissions will give the legislative and executive branches allowances of currency, resources, and sustenance for use in international aid. If extra allowances are sought, the Supreme Court of Governmental Affairs will again resolve any resulting conflict.

Inventions and New Products

Inventions, Step By Step: On paper, a citizen invents an improved carburetor and pays a minimal fee to submit it to the Patent Office. The patent is granted. For another small fee, the inventor submits the idea to the Office of Product Selection (of the Conglomerate of Commercial and Industrial Operations—CCIO). Upon final clearance, the invention is accepted and the contract is signed. The carburetor is then developed, refined, and its individual parts are drafted for production (Division of Research and Development). An actual unit is built and the Product Inspection Agency is notified, which certifies the carburetor as compatible with safety and emission standards. The item is now ready for mass production.

The Office of Facilities Allotment (OFA) finds no adequate commercial manufacturing concerns available; therefore, it assigns governmental staff and facilities to forge the individual parts. The resources are obtained from the Office of Resource Management and the components are manufactured by the Division of Commercial Production. The OFA finds private concerns who will receive the components and assemble the finished units. The Office of Quality Control will randomly inspect both the individual parts before they leave the Conglomerate and the completed units before they leave the commercial assemblers. The units are cleared, and the private assemblers are paid per unit produced.

The units are shipped to the Product Marketing Agency (PMA), which finds dealers to handle the marketing. The units are sold wholesale to the dealers on a limited refundable basis, wherein they will be sold to consumers—also on a limited refundable basis. Once the wholesale refund-deadline has transpired for a designated amount of sales, the applicable royalties will be released to the inventor, and the Conglomerate's production cost for that quantity of units will be marked "paid." The PMA will utilize the Citizens' Advertising Agency and the Citizens' Media Network in order to advertise the carburetor's availability to the general public. The inventor may also offer sales deals in the marketplace but must ensure that prices are set to cover Conglomerate production costs.

Years pass; obsolescence serves to deplete the carburetor's marketability, and production is halted. The dealers lower their prices or return all refundable units to the PMA. (All unsold <u>non</u>refundable units will be resold to the Conglomerate at scrap-metal rate, where they will be converted into other products or auctioned off.) All returned, refundable units will then be sold on consignment through commissioned dealers, wherein the price will be lowered as needed in order to attract sales. Royalties will be paid in an amount proportional to prices, and the dealers will keep records of all sales. Once the price reaches scrap-metal value, the units are returned to the Conglomerate and recycled or auctioned. All Conglomerate economic losses will be subsidized by the government, but prices will be engineered to provide the excess projected to be needed to cover the production cost of unsold items.

The above illustrates the significant amount of governmental aid that will be available to the creators of products of significant social benefit. Creators with ideas of lower impact will seek the commercial sector for aid in executing all steps other than patenting. Whatever the case, the most ecologically and socially beneficial products will be given superior priority. The governmental and commercial sectors will be governmentally compelled to utilize and/or convert to the utilization of all new inventions, products, or processes that are ecologically and sanitarily superior and that provide a greater preservation of money and natural resources. The government will also exercise the right to utilize such discoveries and innovations at its discretion with or without the creators' consent but must adequately compensate all private creators. It will also exercise said right regarding all inventions of significant technological advancement—with the intent being that no entity will ever be allowed to gain any technological advantage that could potentially overthrow governmental control or subjugate the citizenry under a private technocracy. All products must pass the safety standards of the Product Inspection Agency. All international trading will be conducted through the International Trade Agency concerning commercial trade.

Jurisprudence

Criminal court proceedings will center around finding truth rather than the pitting of one side against the other for the objective of winning cases more so than dispensing justice. At no time will any defendant be subjected to any proceeding that puts him or her at the mercy of possible corruption resulting from prosecutors pressured to land convictions. Criminal court legal structure will consist of an investigative team, a judge, an inquiry panel, and jurists (on an optional basis), with attorneys for the defense and prosecution being present but not prominent in proceedings.

First, the defending and prosecuting attorneys will each file a detailed report regarding the case to the court. The investigative team will then work outside the courtroom gathering and verifying all info and evidence regarding the filed reports and present it to the judge and inquiry panel. The function of the judge is self-explanatory. The inquiry panel will dictate the inquiries instead of the attorneys. The panel will consist of a varied quantity of individuals possessing the necessary skills relevant to understanding the particular case at hand. Panel members will ask questions to the defendant and witnesses, with the intent being to compare answers in order to determine the most likely course of events that actually occurred. The panel will be the entity rendering the verdict unless the defendant desires a jury. (Optional: After the panel has completed its inquisition, the jury will be granted the chance to present the panel with a written account of any additional questions the jury members feel haven't been answered, whereupon the trial will be continued until those issues have been cleared. The jury then renders the verdict.) Defense and prosecuting attorneys may be present in the courtroom, but only to serve as advisors to the defendant and plaintiff. However, after the inquiry panel has completed its questioning, the attorneys may submit written questions for the panel to ask before the end of the trial.

Criminal indictments will be handled in the same manner as criminal-court proceedings.

Civil court will consist of the standard setup of a judge, attorneys for both sides, and jurists.

Land

Via the Land Allotment Commission: The vast majority of the nation's land must be set aside, never to be disturbed, as wilderness, havens for wildlife, and as nature's stock for maintaining ecological balance and purity. Of the remaining land (that will be legally exploitable by man), all land for governmental usage is then bound off and accounted for. Land is then accounted for that shall be controlled by the individual citizens who are intended to be completely upheld by the semisocialist system according to the population limit; land is then set aside for population expansion if the limit has not been reached. Of the civilian land, sections may be divided as to residential and commercial zones for traffic purposes. Lastly, land is set aside for emergencies and extras such as disaster shelters, religious structures, community places, concert halls, sporting stadiums, museums, etc. The people of the various locales will be allowed to vote on the usage of some of this extra land. In order to maintain a secure and definite amount of land, none of it is to be sold to foreigners on a private basis.

All exploitable civilian land is to be accounted for by bonds that are distributed by the government (Department of Land Management). Each citizen will be represented by two lateral sections of land (granted property lots—GPLs) and will be given a limit of two land bonds upon their request after reaching adulthood and after completing the nation's minimum education requirements (a high school diploma plus a college or trade school degree, unless granted special dispensation by the government), wherein they become "land representatives." They may utilize their properties in any legal manner desirable, with the intent being to allow them a lateral property for residence and a lateral one for business. No individual may buy or sell additional lots, but the trading of lots with the government or with other land representatives will be allowed, and citizens may be paid to trade or may rent multiple lots from multiple representatives.

Minimum-Wage Enforcement

The legislature and the president will set and monitor the minimum wage based upon constitutional guidelines and the related economic atmosphere. (Perhaps a good rule of thumb would be to set the minimum wage so that one individual could comfortably support a spouse and two children.) The government will automatically adhere to the rate concerning its lowest-paid employees. Entrepreneurs desiring the government's incentives will be required to sign an agreement making them liable to fines and/or exclusion from incentives upon violation of the wage rate. Money from fines will be distributed among the employees of the guilty businesses. Bosses and employees may keep pay receipts for the protection of their interests. (Note: The minimum wage will include enough to cover the surcharge on essentials so that low-income earners effectively pay no taxes out of pocket when meeting their basic needs.)

Penal Matters

All facilities of incarceration will be controlled and operated by the government (Department of Law Enforcement), and the prisoners will be humanely housed and treated. Rehabilitative procedures will be practiced according to offense committed. All prisoners will work either in the maintenance of the facility or on items brought into it, with the earnings going to the victims, to the prisoners and their families, and to the maintenance of the facility. The work may be done for a commercial concern or for the government. Commercial concerns will be given incentives—such as free advertising—to hire ex-offenders.

All inmates will have access to a library and to educational facilities throughout their incarceration and will be allowed to obtain collegiate or technical degrees. Any inmate considered capable of being rehabilitated who invents or discovers anything that will benefit mankind will have their sentence suspended or will have it reduced by an amount proportional to the significance of their contribution. All such creators who are considered incapable of being rehabilitated will remain confined but will be awarded in other manners such as a transfer to a more amiable facility designed especially for these achievers. Upon release, all will be provided with jobs in various locations throughout the nation.

All juvenile detention facilities will be controlled and operated by the government (Division of Child Supervision), wherein the juveniles' education will be continued, rehabilitative therapies and exercises practiced, and wherein the length of detention will be set according to severity of crime.

Population Control

As said, the Constitution will establish the ultimate population limit, never to be increased. It will be based on the maximum amount of exploitable land that can be used by man without danger of detrimental ecological side effects. In order to maintain accurate population counts, citizen registration cards will be issued (by the National Census Agency) that all must possess if they are to secure and maintain government employment or are to receive free governmental services. During all times, new products and birth control devices will be rigorously sought so that the possibility of unwanted pregnancy will be diminished. Such devices sold by the government will be distributed as cheaply as possible to the populace. Also, reversible operations and surgical implants will be developed to allow citizens to turn their reproductive capabilities on an off.

The Department of Population Control will refer to data from the National Census Agency in order to determine the extent to which population control will be enforced. Enforcement will be based on a series of stages:

1st Stage (slowly approaching limit)— Economic incentives and penalties concerning procreative self-control will begin to be enforced; a limit on children will be set, whereby those monetary incentives and penalties will take effect. Those parents who obey the limit will continue to garner all privileges that the semisocialist system has to offer. For every child born in excess of the limit, the parents will be commanded to pay a significant portion of their income for these services—if necessary, by the garnishing of their wages or by other official mandates that dictate that they pay. However, they may take the option of patronizing the private sector for the services if they wish to avoid governmental intervention. Also in the 1st stage, immigration is curtailed.

2nd Stage (rapidly approaching limit)— Forced sterilization will begin for over-productive parents. No further immigrants are allowed unless they are political refugees of extreme need.

3rd Stage (limit reached)— All children born above the limit will be sterilized. No refugees of any type accepted. (Consider this extreme? Read "Population Control" in "SEMISOCIALIST MORALITY & PRINCIPLES.")

Prostitution (Consensual Adult)

Legal if practiced discretely and out of normal public view. May not be practiced in any domain that is also occupied by minors. (Hopefully, a fair and just socioeconomic system would greatly diminish anyone's desire to participate in the world's oldest profession.)

Resources

All raw resources are to be extracted, stored, processed, sold, internationally exchanged, and recycled by the government: Department of Resource Management (extraction, international exchange); Division of Resource Distribution (storage, selling); Division of Civil and Governmental Production (processing, recycling); Division of Commercial Production (processing). The government will function as the major processor and recycler of resources because of the substantial facilities required and because of elaborate pollution control; all unsold products will eventually be recycled. The Division of Resource Distribution will sell the resources to other governmental offices, the civilian sector, and to commercial businesses that may turn them into finished goods. The Resource Allotment Commission will serve as the regulator in order to maintain a balance of distribution between the sectors. The RAC will staff economists, business and political experts, and scientists who will examine all incoming reports in order to execute the most beneficial allotment of the nation's resources. Its goals will be to avoid a dominant military industrial complex, eliminate all threats of oligarchic or monopolistic resource buyouts, and to ensure the general public of adequate access to exploitable resources.

Retirement and Elderly Age

There will be no mandatory retirement age, but a standard age—that will rise as life expectancy rises—will be set for official purposes. Forced retirement will be based upon proven incompetency. Voluntary retirement will be based upon reaching the standard age and the individual's decision as to whether or not enough funds have been accumulated for a comfortable lifestyle. The Department of Seniority will retain enough projected funds (Senior's Retirement Fund) to mail all retirees a monthly basic subsistence check; the citizens may also choose to store money for retirement in savings accounts throughout their working lives.

Revenue

All revenue acquired by the government will be derived from its marketing of goods and services (sustenance, utilities, resources and fuels, transportation, rent, postal services, production and marketing services, bank loans, bonds) and from fines and penalties. A surcharge will be added onto the production and/or operating costs of these commodities (bonds excluded) of an amount capable of maintaining governmental operations. The National Reserve will set the surcharge rate—which will be based upon: 1) the amount of revenue needed to operate the government's essential and significantly beneficial services (with their level of importance dictating the amount of funding allotted by the Reserve), 2) the amount of saleable goods and services the government produces that are projected to be completely consumed by the populace in an indexed amount of time, and 3) the excess charge on those said goods and services that will generate that said amount of revenue in that same indexed time. All governmental offices will automatically receive all funding to purchase all allotments granted to them by the allotment agencies. The surcharge rate will be elastic. Because revenue-collection will be a constant process, it will allow the flexibility that, in the event of an under- or an oversupply of revenue, the surcharge can be raised or lowered at any time; surcharges can also be altered on any particular commodities. All civil governmental offices will purchase from the Reserve at production and/or operating costs—no surcharge added since it is a need of the people. When remunerative acts are performed by government for private concerns (example: CCIO), the full surcharge rate will be imposed, with the costs being passed on to the private concerns or to consumers. (Note: Areas such as the banking system and the Division of Patents, Trademarks, and Copyrights are of both civil and commercial importance and will also be exempt from surcharges.)

Businesses will be allowed to purchase their applicable sustenance and resources at designated locations in bulk at lower prices in exchange for aiding the Reserve in accurately determining the most sufficient quantity of currency to release into circulation. The allotment agencies will issue business ratings according to business size in order to ensure that allotments granted to each business are proportional to the facilities owned with which to exploit them (to ensure that the discounted commodities are put towards actual business endeavors and aren't simply cordially dispersed). Service-rendering businesses will be rewarded through free and extensive advertising, loan accessibility, and by other means. The businesses will regularly complete informational forms regarding the main monetary aspects of their status and activities. The Reserve will use these forms to determine the rate of growth of the economy so that the amount of currency released will keep a healthy pace.

Example of bulk purchasing: Let's say that the surcharge needed for national operations is projected to be 27%. To the general public, a pound of tomatoes that may initially cost $1 (to produce, ship to the Reserve, and in man-hours per pound to sell) would sell from the Division of Sustenance Distribution for $1.27. A particular business helping the Reserve set cash-release/withholding rates (eliminating the usual governmental man-hours needed for stocking and selling, and maybe going a step further by providing its own shipping) would buy the tomatoes in bulk for, let's say, $1.08 per pound (85¢ plus 27% surcharge).

As the private sector increasingly markets its allowable essential goods and services to the public, the governmental market in these will shrink, and less and less revenue will be needed. Thus, the surcharge rate will decrease for all citizens—thereby increasingly allowing them more of a choice between the private and governmental sectors.

I'd like to add that research and development marketed to foreigners (as supplied by the CCIO) would also be a great method for raising revenue. Instead of relying mostly on physical resources, a nation can educate its people, making them intellectual resources. This generates another tremendous advantage: Foreigners "export" their ideas to you. They relay that knowledge to you so that you may transform it into a marketable product.

Sports

The government will support and provide all activities and facilities surrounding sporting endeavors at governmental schools and institutions. Private and commercial concerns will either use sporting facilities on land awarded to them by vote or will rent governmental facilities.

Governmental college athletes will be eligible for pay via the National Collegiate Athletic Fund (two separate funds for the two genders), that will encompass various funds in the various sports into which the general populace may contribute and that will then distribute the pay evenly to all such athletes at the end of their sport's season. The different divisions of colleges will have separate funds. If possible, the government will operate its athletic program on a break-even basis with ticket sales alone; monies generated from sales of broadcast rights to the commercial media and from sales of team logo paraphernalia will be contributed directly into that particular sport's athletic fund unless it is needed by the government to cover operating costs. Athletes will be allowed to endorse goods.

No governmental grade-school or collegiate coach's salary will exceed that of the average salary of a teacher or professor of equal seniority. Separate athletic funds could be established into which supporters could contribute "bonus pay" to all coaches equally.

Sustenance

The government (Department of Sustenance) will control and operate all major farmland and all massive endeavors dealing with the production, raising, and capturing of crops and livestock that serve to feed the nation and that will be traded internationally. All crops will be all-natural—no genetically altered types, no unnecessary chemicals. (Hydroponics will be in high use, along with purified water.) The government (Division of Sustenance Distribution) will operate all emporiums that sell all edible sustenance in its pure or raw state. The Sustenance Allotment Commission will perform the same function with sustenance as the RAC does with resources. Individual citizens wishing to farm one or both of their GPLs or form farming co-ops on multiple GPLs may do so but only for their own consumption and/or to give away; they may sell food that is only in a cooked or processed state. (You can't sell the apple, but you can sell the applesauce.)

The commercial sector may purchase the raw edibles from the government and convert them into original products to sell to the public; commercial markets, restaurants, bakeries, ice cream stores, and other such establishments will buy their needed raw ingredients from the government. The commercial sector will control the market in such items as soaps, furniture polish, deodorants, mouthwash, etc., and will also control it in all finished edible products such as bread, cakes, pizza, cereal, and snack food. Aesthetic crops such as flowers, shrubbery, and ferns will be completely commercially controlled. Also, the raising and selling of pets will be a purely capitalistic endeavor. Private concerns wanting high volume may turn to the government (Division of Commercial Sustenance Production) for production of their finished food products if said products are judged as worthy by the Office of Product Selection.

Transportation

All major forms of the nation's domestic and international transportation patronized by the general public will be governmentally controlled and operated (Department of Transportation). The Division of Transportation Collection will sell all tickets and collect all such monies.

The commercial sector may not compete with the government on any large scale. It may provide transportation to the general public, but only through the use of vehicles oriented towards the more specific locations where the government's broader roster doesn't reach. The sector will completely control all taxis and limousines, car rental services, cruise ships, and all joyrides.

Utilities

All utilities sold to the populace and the facilities that produce them are to be controlled and operated by the government. The populace will purchase them according to their rate of usage.

Water Access (Recreational)

Docks available for rent from the government. The bigger the boat, the bigger the rent. Regarding lakes, rivers, ponds, and streams, no motorized aqua vehicles will be allowed that significantly disturb wildlife or the environment. The Coast Guard will regulate and police all oceanic activity, with the Department of the Interior managing the inner waters.

SEMISOCIALISM'S ADVANTAGES OVER CAPITALISM

1) Land Equalization Factor— Equal land distribution is constant fair-wealth distribution. The desire for business expansion would compel successful entrepreneurs to seek out and compensate more and more representatives for the use of their land. Prosperity by some thusly brings prosperity to others.

2) Valued Currency— The nation's currency has automatic value because it's backed by the resources and services the government controls and renders.

3) Limitation of Aristocratic Power— The aristocracy will forever be denied a private takeover of the nation's infrastructure. The nation always belongs to the masses.

4) Security of Revenue— No one can cheat the government or evade contributing to its pool of revenue because of the universal need for government-controlled services and goods. Also, revenue growth and private growth go hand in hand; the larger a commercial concern grows, the more government-controlled resources and services it will consume.

5) Productivity of Revenue— Because the government will control the resources and utilities and will be providing its own goods and performing its own services, there will be no private concerns inflating the prices for profit and thereby siphoning off the nation's revenue base. This will greatly reduce the cost of necessities for the public, allowing more money for nonessential (free-market) spending.

6) Profitability of Secured Survival— The nation's revenue is released to the support structure first, then to the free-market arena. This secured survival spurs high consumer confidence. (If I know that the economic system is designed to give my survival priority over all other human concerns, yes, I'll use my extra pocket money to buy that vase or painting you're selling.) Also, because they will not be required to pay life-sustaining benefits (such as pensions and health insurance), employers will be more enthusiastic about hiring full-time help.

7) Hospitality of Revenue Collection— The pay-as-you-go method of revenue collection relieves all headaches associated with keeping records, making the act of conducting business a breeze. (Just set up and sell one's product or service. If one wishes to forego the governmental incentives associated with helping the Reserve determine economic growth, there is no bookkeeping required other than the amount needed to conduct one's business.) Also, the nation will reap enormous savings due to the elimination of the need for auditors, accountants and lawyers.

8) The Hospitality of Innovation— Technology will be economically progressive rather than destructive toward opportunity, never eliminating the common man's economic livelihood in favor of automation. Once a benevolent and/or ecologically superior technology is discovered or created, everyone will be compelled to adopt it—if necessary, through governmental subsidies. These constant changes will continuously need personnel to implement and maintain them and thereby should prevent "technological abandonment" (downsizing) of the national workforce. The workers will be trained, retrained, or transferred to other employment in order to ensure that these conversions are as painless as possible. Also, government will use technology, particularly automation, to increasingly reduce the work hours of

its workers, yet allow them to maintain their same salaries. Thus, they can chase after more money elsewhere or they can have more time for human and recreational interaction. Plus, the more products technology creates, the more resources exploited, the more revenue created to further lower living costs.

9) Enforceable Environmental Laws— Because government will have more control over the nation's sustenance, resources, environment, and the industrial incorporation of these, the greed factor (characteristic of the private sector) will not impede prudent judgment regarding monetary expenditures on environmental protection and purification.

10) Rising Standard of Living— Because the factors of fair land-access, economic equity, stability of currency, and population control will be in action, the nation's socioeconomic infrastructure will be stabilized and will be increasingly complimented with gains in its quantity of necessities and luxuries as the government uses technological advancement to continuously lower living costs by making production, resource use, and service-rendering more efficient.

11) Secured Retirement Benefits— The aging crisis—as a threat to retirement benefits—is reduced because the cost of living will be continuously reduced. (Also, the retirement age will be increased proportionately as life spans increase.)

SEMISOCIALIST'S ANSWER TO SOCIALISTS

Greetings socialist cousins,

There are those of you who would denounce capitalism in all its forms, proclaiming that it should be abolished from the world forever—never to surface again to drag man to the immoral depths of exploitation and predation. I agree that capitalism, in its present world-system form, has been ruthlessly and malignantly applied. But there is a correct way that it can be implemented in order to make it probably the most stimulating and invigorating force for furthering human advancement and prosperity—while also making it virtually completely beneficial to the masses in the process, with absolutely no detrimental side effects whatsoever regarding society's socioeconomic stability.

Capitalism <u>done</u> <u>right</u> is capitalism subjugated under socialism. I define myself as a "semisocialist"—one advocating the socialist distribution of the essentials and the free-market distribution of the nonessentials or luxuries. Under the semisocialist system, an elected government controls the essential resources and services, markets some of them to the citizenry at a surcharged (taxed) rate, and then releases the revenue toward the needs and advancement of the people before releasing any currency to the free-market arena. Some of that said advancement will include technological innovations that will free citizens from the drudgeries of labor and that will continuously lower living costs due to cheaper production techniques and materials, allowing people to spend less time being drones and more time being with family and friends and enjoying the amenities this world has to offer—what life should <u>really</u> be like for Earth's children.

Yes, socialism is basically a noble socioeconomic system promoting the better side of man. But we all know that the better side of man hasn't won out in the course of human existence. Somehow, during man's social, economic, and political endeavors, greed, vanity, exploitation, environmental abuse, and racism have surfaced from his genes to produce a resulting world of poverty, pollution, war and hatred, and egoistic materialism in the face of socioeconomic disparity. Somehow, the result of all human effort has been the ability of these defiled traits to produce the world we live in today.

These traits are destructive and negative, but they did indeed develop—for some reason that we may or may not comprehend. These are of the universal truths and cosmic realities that shape man's destiny. Thus, any governmental system adopted for the purpose of improving humanity's plight must acknowledge these truths and realities and incorporate them in a constructive manner rather than "ignore them" ("ignorantly placing bandages on the effect rather than cures on the cause") and allowing them to surface and plague humanity in unexpected and deleterious manners. This is what semisocialism does and what I'm afraid socialism will not do in all cases.

Semisocialism's master ingredient (evolutionarily constructive revenue distribution) is the key factor that accommodates the constructive incorporation of these aforementioned traits—in actuality, transforming most of them into positive contributors to societal advancement. Greedy people want more money. In their pursuit of it, they tend to establish more commercial concerns and consume more resources, therefore expending more capital. In the semisocialist system, since government controls the raw resources and main services they need, the resulting increase in collected revenue allows for more constructive governmental action that is beneficial to the masses. Vanity (egotistic monetary expenditure) is constructively incorporated in this manner as well. Also, when a government is dedicated to ecological preservation—pollution control, alternative energy, recycling—more monetary resources are available for that. Plus, more entrepreneurs will join the ecological train when government-sponsored economic incentives are provided that compel them to do so. The potential for unfair economic exploitation dissipates as government makes more capital available for small businesses and as an expanding economy is generated from equitable economic distribution and also generated from progressive technology that continuously lowers the cost of living. Racism is basically the institutional impedance of one sector of the people for the benefit of another sector of the people. Both socialism and semisocialism keep this abomination in check through equitable resource distribution that doesn't allow one sector unfair socioeconomic advantage over another.

Semisocialism allows people to gainfully act on their greedy and materialistic tendencies. Greed isn't all bad; it also has the propensity to spur creativity and effort. This is the definition of merit. People have a right to prosper according to merit. And they <u>should</u> <u>not</u> be held back by being forced to endure equality with those less motivated and accomplished than themselves. Understand, class distinction <u>isn't</u> the problem; class subjugation <u>is</u>. Semisocialism's main safety factor against class subjugation: equal land distribution. This safety factor will prevent one economic class from inordinately acquiring the <u>main</u> earthly base that contains the essential resources everyone needs in order to survive. Higher classes will develop only from money left over <u>after</u> the needs of the people have been met—mainly because "luxury money" will not be released to the capitalist arena by government until it is so. Thus, you can indeed merge the two systems of socialism and capitalism by establishing two separate support bases—one based upon sustaining the nation and citizenry (the primary economy) and the other based upon establishing and expanding the free market (secondary economy). The secondary economy helps feed the primary one, while the primary economy regulates the secondary one.

"From each according to ability, to each according to need." Again, merit is the problem here. Some people are highly motivated while others are just plain lazy. I know this, and, deep down, I believe my socialist world relatives know this as well. The "from each" people have to produce in order for the "to each" people to have something to meet their needs. In order for things to be fair, every capable individual must contribute an adequate amount. Otherwise, what's to stop the candlestick maker from giving one candle to society while taking a diamond from it? Thus, one's quantity of work hours, tasks completed, or products contributed must be tracked and recorded in order to ensure that fairness persists. And if you have someone's work-hours, tasks or products documented, you might as well have <u>money</u>.

There is absolutely nothing wrong with money. It is the unfair and/or inadequate distribution of it that is the villain. A system of currency allows people to work now and store their spending potential until the exact time that they wish to expend it. Money in one's hand allows one to be mobile and acquire anything at any place at any time. It allows exact exchange for exact value. And, most relevant to this topic, it allows merit to determine the quantity of goods and services—particularly those in excess of the essential ones—that everyone receives. Thus, if you desire only the basic life, then you put in your minimum effort and reap the minimum rewards. If you want the good life, then you put forth the good effort. Money is both the motivator and the documenter. Also understand, there are people who just don't want to work all their lives. They want to go for the gold early and get out of the rat race early, to spend half or more of their lives traveling the world, seeing the sites, and having fun. The capitalist aspect—the monetary accumulation aspect—of semisocialism allows everyone the opportunity for early cessation from labor upon adequate economic accumulation. And this type of idleness is not the devil's workshop—especially if they accumulated the wealth by inventing the better mousetrap that advances the world's capabilities or if they simply just contributed to greater production that spurs increase in society's monetary circulation.

Finally—and most practically regarding your point of view, my socialist friends—there is the issue concerning just how on earth you plan on getting a politically empowering amount of First-Worlders to switch from the extreme of a market-based society to that of a socialist-based one. (Of course, this isn't to say that you couldn't work with the less developed world regions in order to build your base.) It is illogical, and very naive, to believe that the jump from "me, myself, and I" to "us, ourselves, and we" will be made in one fell swoop, with absolutely no transitional stage occurring in-between. Semisocialism is the perfect instrument to serve as the buffer for the complete conversion. In my opinion, if semisocialism were adopted, there would be few individuals desiring to convert from it to pure socialism. But, for those who would, it would serve the imperative function of eliminating the socialists' archenemy (the private sector) from control of the life-sustaining essentials while simultaneously pacifying these lucre-minded entrepreneurs with a free-market base from which they may prosper. A semisocialist system would better put the whole of society into a socialist mood, getting everyone used to socialism's essential ingredients and fostering an atmosphere more congenial to politically and systematically accommodating complete socialist conversion for those desiring it. Socialists could then push for policies allowing for their proportional control of the resources, wherein they could establish and develop their own socioeconomic support base, sustaining their members' livelihood. If said support base accommodates all their members' needs, then they could retain all gains made from their labors. However, if they still depend upon the semisocialist system for any essentials, then they would contribute resources, finished products, or labor (since socialists reject the use of currency) to the semisocialist government in the adequate proportion. Socialists would be on their own as far as orchestrating their mediums and methods for rewarding labor. And multiple systems for criminal/civil law and the military could be established that would allow socialists legal autonomy regarding their internal affairs and that allow them to voluntary contribute to national defense—with the philosophy being that, if there are people who don't think enough of their nation to defend it, then they accept the fact that they could lose it.

Thus, just as semisocialism allows socialism and capitalism to coexist, so, too, does it allow the coexistence of socialism and semisocialism itself.

ESTABLISHING THE SEMISOCIALIST SYSTEM

I believe "How will we establish a system <u>within</u> a system?" is the most practical question here. As we all know that there is virtually no such thing on Earth as instantaneous transformation from right to left...or vice versa—that is, not unless the "would-be conquerors" are equipped with the necessary armament to immediately overwhelm the existing powers that be. And, understand—<u>thoroughly</u> and <u>passionately</u>—it will NEVER be the way of the semisocialist to "wage war" against any nation's authority or to even instigate inflammatory conflict. Such a thing puts one at odds with officialdom empowered with the might to extinguish one in one's infancy as well as with the legionary lemmings of the order who obey and protect their systematic masters...whether going over the cliff or not So, the main focus is to design, create, and enact "subsystems" that elevate one's socioeconomic status while also ameliorating as many difficulties and deficiencies as possible in the process.

Once established and made massively known to the general populace, the new system's own inherent superiorities would automatically assert themselves as a force to be reckoned with and as an existing, formidable, alternative to the defective standard structure in place. Plus, the fact that all participants are comprised by individuals who <u>voluntarily</u> submitted to the new structure, and were in no way <u>coerced</u>, eliminates any and all grounds for "justified" retaliation from old-world-order boys and girls who must acknowledge change is coming—change not of their own making, not of their own "perfect world" conceptions. Most "traumatically," these people would have to come to grips with the fact that there's a <u>new</u> kid in town—one who's collectively oriented and one who puts new light on the adage, "I am my brother's keeper."

Organizing

In order for semisocialism to serve as our platform for change, an official organization would be necessary so that the overall movement would be readily identifiable and in the forefront of the eyes of the masses...bearing a name such as "Semisocialist Coalition," "World Semisocialist Coalition" (or "Association"), "Semisocialist United Front," etc.

To avoid tax burdens (and possible systematic attack via antagonistic tax-collection forces), the organization may benefit most by being "informal" and charging no membership fees or accepting donations. It's main purpose would be to serve as a means for allowing members to connect and network. Thus the organizing officials themselves must be in a position allowing them to work without compensation. Members would network most effectively via the organization's Web site, which could be funded by multiple members willing to collaborate to pay all expenses...or by a singular one possessing the means. People would have to join the organization in order to take advantage of semisocialist-provided savings and opportunities, with each receiving an official membership card and ID #. Individuals wishing to give patronage but not join would be charged more for goods/services. To discourage those who would join for benefits more so than ideological allegiance, the stipulation would be that, should any existing/former member later oppose the semisocialist cause in a significant manner, he/she would be publicly exposed as hypocritical and insecure in his/her ideological belief.

Leadership

Before any journey to socioeconomic independence can ever begin, there must be clear and present leadership available to direct the members onto the course set by the semisocialist model. That being the case, some form of electoral process must be conducted to select the best and brightest. I, myself, feel that the best way to manage this would be to list all salient needs humans require to exist and flourish and then allow respondents, desiring to develop the system to supply said needs, to state how they would satisfy them and what resources/talents they now posses to accomplish this. From the pool of said respondents, the general membership would select the best candidates as leaders.

Once the leaders are selected, members could network and contribute their talents toward meeting the needs of the collective body by advancing any available projects. And, since a collective body is best nourished via collective control, all endeavors of an industrial nature should be co-op oriented, whereby joint ownership is the order and all members have a major voice in determining direction in a structure designed to benefit all.

Any profits acquired in access of operating costs would go toward expansion of the industrial base as well as toward advancing technological capabilities that allow production to become increasingly cheaper so that member consumers can retain more and more of their wealth—and thus become the exemplary force for world change. A portion of it would also be invested into a general fund for the purpose of funding other social needs.

To forever prevent obscene wage disparity, no leader (CEO) should ever be paid more than 10 times the wage of that industry's lowest-paid full-time employee.

General Fund

A general fund would be necessary in order to establishment/operate our social programs. The fund could be started as a non-profit organization, with an officially registered name. A portion of the profits earned from all profit-making industries would be contributed into the fund.

Industry & Commerce (Profit-Making)

Goal: To satisfy the industrial/commercial needs/wants of membership and nonmembership consumers at low cost while continuously lowering costs further via technological and systematic advancements. Profits generated via cost-only or minimal-profit prices charged to members and higher prices to nonmembers. ULTIMATE OBJECTIVE: To expand globally to the point where further expansion is no longer necessary and only the continuous lowering of pricing via advancing capabilities is the remaining goal.

Agriculture: Potential land is any ready agrarian area as well as any land adequate enough to accommodate hydroponic activity and/or the raising of livestock. As much as possible, to keep crops maintained in their natural state, the Frankenstein monster should be prevented from infiltrating the genetic strain. Co-op commerce would most economically be conducted via semisocialist-establish markets, traveling vendors, and mail order when possible.

Banking: Everyone knows bankers rule the world. Let's therefore get the people to put the money into <u>our</u> hands so that we can manage finances the <u>right</u> way. Special emphasis would be placed on making loans to green/fair-trade applicants. Also, money donated from the general fund would be used for low-interest home loans for members and as grants to help sustain any semisocialist-controlled profit-making industries needing extra capital to maintain operations.

Construction: Houses, buildings and other structures made from eco/energy-efficient/noncombustible materials as much as possible. Provided via salaried personnel building and selling completed structures for cost-only to members and for fair market value to nonmembers.

Energy: Goal: To establish a renewable-energy network comprised of production (solar, wind, etc.) as well as distribution (batteries, EV charging-stations/batteries, direct home connection).

Insurance: Categories: Health/Dental, Vehicular, Home, Business/Professional. Operated by salaried personnel.

Manufacturing: Various categories accommodated: Metallic, Plastic/Synthetic, Wooden, Chemical, Electronic, Electrical, Fabric/Sartorial, Paper/Cardboard, etc. Practicing eco-social responsibility, manufacturers operate on a low-profit basis for members and a higher one for nonmembers.

Marketing/Commerce: Marketing facilities and Websites offering discount prices to members and competitive prices to nonmembers. Emphasis on eco-social responsibility.

Shipping: Categories: Land, Air, Sea. Major goal would be to convert to electric vehicles as well as improve air-shipping efficiency. Emphasis on recyclable packaging.

(Other industries: Travel, Entertainment, Packaging, etc. could be included later.)

Social Programs (Requiring Funding)

Goal: To satisfy the social needs of the members and nonmembers at low cost while continuously lowering costs further via technological and systematic advancements. Cost-only fees charged to members and higher fees to nonmembers. ULTIMATE OBJECTIVE: Same as that of Industry & Commerce.

Health Care: Accommodated best via the establishment of co-op medical facilities, wherein all personnel are salaried and operations are on a break-even basis for members as well as nonmembers—thus completely eliminating the profit motive. The general fund would help subsidize financial difficulties. (Thus, health care would require funding only if necessary.)

Education: Accommodated best via grants and/or low-interest loans to members regarding tuition for essential majors (medical, scientific/ engineering/technical, legal, etc.) taught in existing institutions. (Though eventually, semisocialist-controlled educational facilities could be established, practicing more sound policies than existing, standard, institutions.)

Housing (Affordable): (Serving only members.) Accommodated best via the establishment of a semisocialist-controlled charitable house-building organization operating at break-even, whereto the general fund could contribute, members/general-public could make donations, and whereby governmental grants could be acquired. General fund would subsidize if necessary.

Elderly Security: Members join a retirement plan allowing them invest in semisocialist industrial development and receive dividends upon retirement. Will be an individual fund subsidized by the general fund as necessary.

Legal Aid (Underprivileged): Accommodated best via donations to existing charitable legal-aid organizations dedicated to helping the lower-income.

Day Care: Accommodated via membership-controlled facilities staffed with salaried personnel.

Once the overall movement is well established, the SUPREME goal is to expand to the point where the socioeconomic system is so stable and formidable that the world's populace would have a choice of following it or of remaining dependent upon the traditional world systems.

LET'S GET ORGANIZED!

Simply put, if you want to be a candidate for "Chief Organizer" of the general semisocialist movement or for a leadership position regarding any industrial or social programs, send your name and contact info to me. Include any info regarding your education, skills/talents. Also include your plans to advance the cause you're interested in. *State what contact info you want displayed for respondents to contact you with. (*This info would be posted on the Web: www.adspread.com/semisocialism.htm.)

Send info to: semisocialist@yahoo.com.

EPILOGUE

In closing, I'd like to say that there are many groups and organizations who "wear the labels" and "wave the flags," but few who are truly grounded in the correct policies that foster real progress and advancement for Earth's inhabitants. Whatever socially benevolent organization you associate yourself with, here are some good policies for all such organizations to follow:

1) When recruiting, target people of all races. There are good and bad people of all races. Seek to build a world of good people. Place your interest in the heart, not in skin color. There are people of different races who will fight for your rights and die alongside of you, and there are people of your own race who will sell you out for a pack of cigarettes.

2) To the best of your ability, avoid conflict. Wars are destructive and eternal. They have shaped the world we live in today. And the world today isn't good. As long as we choose to engage in violence, there will always be violence. Let it end with us and with the groups we associate ourselves with. Don't make violent enemies; instead, make strategic allies. Besides, our enemy is so much better armed than us; that's how they got into power in the first place. Also, we don't need any more political prisoners; we need people on the outside, free to move about so that we can get things done. Don't let satanic forces lure you into petty or individualistic battles. Instead, keep your eyes focused on the real prize: building an organization for socioeconomic and political change. Fight the BIG WAR to change the whole system; leave the little battles—and all their violence and conflict—to the rest of the world. What we have to do is make war impractical by positioning ourselves to where we can refuse to become the subjects of the victors.

3) Spend money strategically. Money is the ULTIMATE WEAPON on Earth. Everything else is just a smokescreen. The elitist sector keeps everyone fighting amongst themselves and then goes after the money and resources. And Japan didn't need bombs to invade—and almost conquer—America's economic system. All they needed were smart businesspeople and smart investments. As much as you can, support the good merchants of the earth and abandon the bad ones. Whenever you can, practice collective economics with your members and your allies. Form co-op markets with one another in order to eliminate the middle man and save as much money as possible. Then progress from there. Form co-op production companies and then co-op resource companies that will allow you to extract raw resources and produce the product as well as market it. Another great advantage would be co-op recycling facilities. (Co-op America is a good practitioner of progressive marketing and spending.)

4) This world is a reprobate world—it is an evil, temporary world put into place to try mankind spiritually until the righteous and eternal spiritual forces assume control. Malignant forces are now in power. Therefore, don't become worldly in motivation or blinded by the flashy images this world dangles in front of your eyes. Such things cause you to become distracted from your real purpose. Don't chase after the toys that society says you must have in order to "be somebody"—because society already has enough "somebodies" depleting resources and screwing up world affairs. Don't let this shallow

endeavor drain your time or your finances so that the Beast can further consume you into his belly.

5) Spend your time building a new world instead of fighting this evil one. **Better to build the evolved world of the future than battle the corrupt world of the present.** Our enemies are well-entrenched. We must pull away, acquiring properties and building our own evolved empires on them. And don't fight to try to save this world. Never forget this simple rule: YOU CANNOT SAVE EVERYBODY! Don't try to change snakes into doves. Let snakes be snakes. They were put here by spiritual forces greater than you, and they will be here until spiritual forces remove them. Find doves who are already doves; these will make strong, dependable allies who are already enlightened with our evolved philosophy and who require little to no persuasion to join you. Work with them to pull away from those who are not enlightened and who are content to remain slaves to this evil world. Granted: your group will be a pond in the sea, but what a grand pond it will be. Once others see how pure your waters are, they will want to join.

6) Keep your eyes and ears open for allies. Write down the names and contact information of anyone you hear who espouses socialist– or semisocialist-like values. Always keep a long list of people you can constantly contact to so that you can keep strengthening your argument as to how socialist policies can be implemented in the world. Plus more, as you share with them, they'll share with you.

Whatever we liberal-minded folks do, WE MUST BECOME ORGANIZED! This is why we're getting the socks beat off of us. The right wing is organized. The reason they can organize so easily is simple: Their only platform is "keep the power out of the hands of the masses and in the hands of the few." This goal is tacit but all too apparent. It doesn't have to be overtly stated. They automatically know what to do. So, everything just falls right into place for them. The world is already set up to accommodate their elitist economics. All they have to do is simply look for the little "code words," join up with the entities uttering them, and then follow the system already set in place for them. "Willie Lynch" economics works just like "Willie Lynch" racism.

The world isn't set up to accommodate our righteous economics. So, we have to work harder, building a system to make it happen for us. The more of us who "leave the world" and work together to accomplish this, the easier it will be. We have to organize.

I wish you peace and prosperity in your daily struggles to navigate this world of confusion and controversy.

Toward an evolved world,
Keith B. Anderson

ABOUT MYSELF:

I am a craftsman, amateur writer, and part-time whatever-elser. I'm one who believes that all socioeconomic pains afflicting society can be greatly alleviated upon mankind's adoption of a governmental and economic system incorporating the positives of capitalism (creativity and prosperity) with those of communism or socialism (secured welfare of the masses, equitable resource distribution)—a system I have dubbed "semisocialism."

THIS IS THE MOST IMPORTANT TYPE OF SECULAR BOOK THAT CAN EVER BE WRITTEN!!!

I say this boldly and loudly because it is the ultimate in truth, and it is critically essential that mankind hears such messages now so that it may gradually shift to a more fair and balanced world system before this present one leads us all irretrievably down a dark and dirty road. The essence of its ultimate truth: **Collective need before private greed.**

It matters not how technically advanced a nation is—how many sophisticated toys and flashy gadgets are in mansions and homes at the moment. If the governmental and socioeconomic foundation of those homes and mansions is built on shaky ground, some day, somehow, it will all collapse, burying the toys, gadgets—and their masters—underneath to rust, rot, and be remembered as "an era bygone."

Capitalism is the shakiest foundation that can ever be, propped up with a patchwork of corrections and supports that continuously need updating and enhancing with ever-greater intensity. Lives become shaped by corporate giants rather than by benevolent and collective democratic planning.

Market forces should not determine the course of human direction. Human welfare should. An "ideal society" is not based upon reckless materialistic acquisition or upon repressive subjugation, but, rather, upon an ever-increasing base of holistic insight subjugated under the natural covenant and grounded in humanitarian priority. Acquire all the knowledge we can, use it to live pristinely on this <u>borrowed</u> planet like we should, treat one another like we should.

Those who understand this are the truly evolved of the world—no matter how many extravagant gadgets that may or may not lie in their toy boxes.

SELECTED BIBLIOGRAPHY

Before the Mayflower— Lerone Bennett Jr.

Brain Fuel— L. A. Peterson, Lucy Wiesend, Richard Wiesend

Dangerous Pursuits— Walter Adams & James W. Brock

Encyclopedia Britannica

Frequently Asked Questions (about socialism)—www.worldsocialism.org/canada/faq.htm

Holy Bible (King James Version)

Nature Knows No Color-Line— J. A. Rogers

Sex and Race (Vol. I, II, III)— J. A. Rogers

The Forgotten Americans— John E. Schwartz and Thomas Volgy

The Population Explosion— Paul R. Ehrlich and Ann H. Ehrlich

The Secrets of the Federal Reserve— Eustace Mullins

The World Almanac And Book Of Facts (2000)— PRIMEDIA Reference Inc.

Webster's New Collegiate Dictionary (1981)

Who Needs the Negro?— Sidney Willhelm

Who Robbed America— Michael Waldman

Who Will Tell the People— William Greider